W9-BSI-946

Ministry on the CUTTING EDGE

Rick Ezell

krégel
RESOURCES

Grand Rapids, MI 49501

Ministry on the Cutting Edge by Rick Ezell

Copyright © 1995 by Rick Ezell

Published by Kregel Resources, an imprint of Kregel Publications, P. O. Box 2607, Grand Rapids, MI 49501. Kregel Resources provides timely and relevant resources for Christian life and service. Your comments and suggestions are valued.

Scripture quotations, unless otherwise noted, are from *The Holy Bible: The New International Version* copyright © 1978 by the International Bible Society. Used by permission of Zondervan Publishing House.

Cover and Book Design: Alan G. Hartman

Library of Congress Cataloging-in-Publication Data
Ezell, Richard.
   Ministry on the cutting edge / Richard Ezell.
      p.   cm.
   1. Pastoral theology. 2. Clergy—Office. I. Title.
BV4011.E94   1995   253—dc20   95-8343
                                                        CIP

ISBN 0-8254-2526-3 (paperback)

              1 2 3 4 5 Printing / Year 99 98 97 96 95

Printed in the United States of America

Contents

Preface

It was a beautiful spring afternoon in Chicago as I was driving home in my blue Honda Accord. I had attended a grueling, two-day seminar on church growth—as though I needed to attend another seminar on church growth. But this seminar was being presented by someone other than a pastor whose church could be described with the prefix "mega"; rather, it was led by a researcher, someone that had gathered information from various surveys and focus groups and random telephone calls of people all over the country. He presented his findings in an interesting and compelling fashion—at least as interesting as one can make a truckload of statistics.

As I turned off the freeway onto a tree-lined boulevard that would lead me through the sprawling western suburb of Chicago that I call home, some thoughts kept ricocheting in my mind. I had been to many seminars of all shapes and sizes and had read books and articles promoting all kinds of methods and mechanics that would assist me in being a better pastor and in leading my church to greater effectiveness. Most, if not all, of those resources were well presented and left me with new information and a new challenge to spark me and my church on to the next level. But, as I reflected on this most recent seminar and on most of the seminars I had attended on ministry effectiveness, a key component was missing—the personal authenticity of the minister. I walked away from some seminars and put down certain books feeling that all I needed for ministry effectiveness was to write a vision statement, plant a church in the right location, provide adequate parking and abundant seating, draft a well-trained music group and a gifted drama team, throw in a small-group ministry, and presto, my church would grow to where people could use the prefix *mega* to describe it. But what about my character and my integrity? Don't these ingredients play a part in pastoral effectiveness? I know that all of the mechanics and methods in leading a church require a great deal of work and managerial skill to pull together. But doesn't an effective ministry require more than an abundance of creativity, long work hours, and responsible delegation? Could I have an effective ministry without being an exceptional talent?

Early in my pastoral training I had heard that the church is the extension of the pastor, and the church will take on the personality of the pastor. More recently it has been reiterated that the pastor is the point man. Those facts are, to a great extent, true. But if the church is an extension of the pastor, if the church takes on the personality of the pastor, and if the church looks to the pastor as the point man, doesn't it stand to reason that the authenticity and private world of the pastor needs to be developed, protected, and promoted?

James Means writes in *Effective Pastors for a New Century*, "God rarely blesses the ministry of those with dubious character, questionable behavior, and unremarkable spirituality. God's blessings normally rest upon those who have their moral, spiritual, and intellectual act together."[1] The blessings of God and the effectiveness of ministry hinge upon the private, personal life of the minister. One cannot get around that fact. Granted, a minister lacking personal authenticity may have pastoral effectiveness, but only for a season. God measures ministry success, like He does one's life, not by the external bang of our charisma but by the internal character of our lives; not by the fluff of our personalities but by the integrity of the heart; not by the momentary sparkle of being in the right place at the right time but by a lifetime of commitment and service to the Master that often is unknown and unannounced on this side of heaven.

I hope as you read *Ministry on the Cutting Edge* that you will understand that I have not raised all the issues nor answered all the questions nor explored all the components of personal authenticity and pastoral effectiveness. My desire is that you will implement the disciplines I have suggested so that you will be encouraged in your present ministry to keep giving your all in the kingdom work. And I want you to develop and maintain your ministry effectiveness for a lifetime. Found in the following pages are some of the disciplines that will unlock your pastoral effectiveness so you can minister on the cutting edge.

ENDNOTES

1. James E. Means, *Effective Pastors for a New Century* (Grand Rapids: Baker Books, 1993), 17–18.

1

Have We Lost the Cutting Edge?

John isn't necessarily brilliant or multitalented. His educational background is not impressive, nor is his social standing. He isn't ugly, but neither would his face grace a magazine cover. But he is making a lasting difference in his world. John is a pastor who makes an impact on hundreds of people each year. His ministry is not just an entertainment type of pseudoministry, but a deep-rooted biblical ministry that meets the needs of hurting people in his community.

His pastoral ministry is the talk of the denomination. He could speak to church leaders every day who inquire about how he implements a growing, dynamic, and life-changing program. He can't handle all the calls. Once a quarter, he gathers with all interested comers to share his insights and visions.

One reason John's ministry is out in front of other ministries is because John lives on the cutting edge of effectiveness. He is a leader who is making a difference in his world. Sure, he receives a lot of cruel and unnecessary darts hurled from jealous onlookers, but that comes with the territory. People who make an impact get attacked from both sides—the world they are changing and the complacent majority who don't understand the impetus, or who are jealous of those making the difference they know they should be accomplishing.]

Jesus intended his followers to live out in front. He did not call us to complacency, he called us to action. He did not beckon us to easy chairs, but to war. He did not summon us to retreat, but to advance. He ordered us to the front lines, not to the rear echelons.

Obviously, all who are called are not making an eternal difference. Why is that? Two men may graduate from the same institution, with the same degree, and the same amount of experience, but produce different results in their jobs. One will prosper and make a difference, the other will falter and fail in apathy and indifference. Two churches in the same community with similar theological doctrines, ministering to the same socio-economic class of people with similar potential may achieve different results. While one flourishes the other barely survives. Why?*The reason is simple. Some people, churches, and businesses lose the cutting edge, not necessarily because of a lack of desire or drive, but simply because they fail to put into practice some of the ingredients that kept them on the forefront in earlier days.

Let's examine this phenomenon. What causes one to lose the cutting edge?

A FAILURE TO CHANGE

Everett Anthony, former director of Metropolitan Missions for the Home Mission Board of the Southern Baptist Convention, related an incident that occurred while he and his wife were traveling through Arkansas. Near Little Rock they saw a sign advertising a cotton museum. Since he grew up on a cotton farm they decided to stop.

After he and his wife browsed through the museum, he asked the curator about a good place to eat. She recommended a place just a hundred yards from the museum. She warned them about the appearance of the building. "The structure is no reflection on the food," she said.

They arrived at what was an old country store. It had imitation brick siding and it hung out over a bayou on stilts. Half of the building was still a country store with sparsely-filled shelves. The other half was a restaurant. It was packed with people. Standing outside in the Arkansas heat were more people waiting for a table. The food was not cheap, but it was outstanding.

Before they left, Everett asked the proprietor, "This is my first time here. Tell me how this happened?"

He responded, "This store has been in my family for over fifty years. When I returned home from Vietnam my dad sold it to me. A few years ago I was going broke trying to keep the general store liquid. The new interstate highway bypassed the town and diverted the traffic away from the store. I knew that if I didn't change I was going to die. So I converted half of the store into a restaurant. Now people drive all the way from Little Rock to eat here. I risked everything I had in this venture. But I discovered a gold mine."

We are living in an exciting age of unprecedented change. *The futurists report that in the fifty years between 1970 and 2020 we will experience change equivalent to that of the last five hundred years. The winds of change have given way to the earthquake of change. The message to us is the same as to the store owner: If we don't change we will die.

We lose the cutting edge when we fail to respond to the changes around us. Michael Kami in his book *Trigger Points* has stated that organizations (and I might add, individuals) that will be effective are those that can make decisions* three times faster than they are doing now. And, just as important, these decisions must be implemented three times faster.[1]

George Barna writes in his book *The Frog in the Kettle* about what life will be like in America in the year 2000 and how leaders must respond to those many changes. His title is based on the well-known story of the frog that is placed in a kettle of boiling water. The frog will immediately jump out because it recognizes a hostile environment. But if you place a frog in a kettle of water at room temperature, it will stay there. If you slowly and gradually increase the temperature of the water the frog won't jump out because he is not aware that the environment is changing. You can continue to turn the heat up until the water is boiling. The poor frog will be boiled too—quite content but nevertheless very dead.[2]

Barna contends that changes in our world are occurring constantly and gradually. Are we sensitive to those changes?

Are we operating as though our environment has remained the same? If we are not responding to the changing world around us, we are losing the cutting edge.

The apostle Paul realized that change was essential to effective ministry when he wrote, "To the Jews I became like a Jew, to win the Jews. To those under the law I became like one under the law (though I myself am not under the law), so as to win those under the law. . . . I have become all things to all men so that by all possible means I might save some" (1 Cor. 9:20–22). This is not a hypocritical, chameleon approach to evangelism. This was Paul's strategy for reaching the world. To be effective he knew that he would have to change in order to find common ground of communicating the gospel.

Several options are available to the twentieth-century Christian leader in responding to change. We can ignore the changes. In doing so we will wither up and die. We can simply react to the changes as they occur. That means we will struggle with the frustration of change occurring so rapidly that we can't seem to catch up. Or we can anticipate the changes and adapt our methods and practices to address them. Consequently we will be sharp and effective and growing—living on the cutting edge.

The only constant in this world is change. That is true for the Christian life too. Change is at the heart of the gospel. What is salvation? The wonderful conversion of an individual from spiritual death to spiritual life. And what is sanctification? It is the progression of the believer from worldliness to godliness. And what is justification? It is the complete change so that one day we will stand before God faultless—just as if we had never sinned.

Granted, no one likes change except a wet baby. Someone once said, "Our dilemma is that we hate change and love it at the same time; what we want is for things to remain the same but get better."

All of us resist change at some level and on some issues. And there are some things we should resist changing, because change does not always translate into "better." Our theology and the foundations of our faith and biblical principles must stay the same, but our methods and practices must respond to the changing culture and times.

Karl Marx said, "Philosophers have only interpreted the world differently; the point is, however, to change it."[3] Jesus informed the early disciples, "You are the salt of the earth. . . . you are the light of the world" (Matt. 5:13–14)* That's His way of instructing us, the Christian leaders, to change the world. We aren't just to call attention to areas of needed change, such as social ills, family crises, economic difficulties, or moral impropriety. We are to change them and, ultimately, the world.

A FAILURE TO RISK

Dr. Bob Cox, dean of the Department of Education at the University of Texas at Tyler, said that most institutions and movements eventually go through three stages.*They begin as risk-takers, then they grow to be caretakers, and eventually they end up as undertakers.[4]

Leaders are no exception.

Ministry on the cutting edge means being a risktaker. It was true of the early believers. Paul and Barnabas, the first missionaries from the church in Antioch, were described as "men who have risked their lives for the name of our Lord Jesus Christ" (Acts 15:26 NASB). These men were willing to wager their lives, so to speak, by laying their lives on the line for the cause of Christ. These early believers were so convinced of human lostness, of the good news of the gospel, and of the necessity of missions and evangelism that they risked both life and limb to carry the old story into new places. There was nothing complacent about them.

General George Patton in a speech to his troops declared, "There is one thing I want you to remember. I don't want to get any messages saying we are holding our position. We are advancing constantly. We are not interested in holding anything except the enemy."

His motto was: "Always take the offensive. Never dig in!"[5]

Ministry that makes an impact can no longer do business as usual. The status quo is nothing to "crow" about. People who only talk about the good old days and how we used to do it will lose their effectiveness. Remember, the seven last words of a dying organization are, "We've never done it that way before."

I have heard plenty recently about never doing it that

way before as I am living out one of the biggest risks of my vocational life. Our church began a Saturday evening worship service with a contemporary style of worship in order to reach nonbelievers in our area. This service offered an alternative worship style and an option for people unable to attend on Sundays. Some of my so-called friends informed me that this was vocational suicide. "If it fails, your leadership and vision for the church will be thwarted," they remarked. My reasoning was that this service provided another opportunity to reach people for Christ and His kingdom. We had to venture forth in faith. And so we did. Not blindly or without testing the marketability in the community, but with thoughtful calculation we stepped forth.

Church leadership has operated far too long on the supposition that if events or ministries are not guaranteed to succeed we won't attempt them. What a sad commentary to a Savior who gave His life for us.

I don't know if our Saturday service will succeed, as the world defines success, by noses and nickels. But I do know that it is challenging this church and this pastor to venture forth in faith and minister as Jesus intended.

A poster stated, "A turtle wouldn't get anywhere if it didn't stick out its neck." What's true for turtles is true for effective Christian leaders. Nothing in life is ever achieved without risks. That's why God is challenging a new generation of leaders, just as He challenged Peter, to get out of the boat, to stick out their necks. Impacting the world requires moving out of the safe and secure environment of the four walls of the church. It demands ministering and working outside of comfort zones.

Comfortable Christianity is easy. Not to risk, not to put one's all on the line is the least threatening approach to ministry. It may leave us unscathed but it will also leave our ministries unused and ineffective. In many instances, the Christian community has become so comfortable it is smothering to death. When are we going to realize that ministry is an adventure based on risk?

A FAILURE TO DREAM

Dreaming is the ability to see beyond today. It is the capacity to anticipate the future. Effective ministry is built on

✳anticipation rather than reaction. Dreamers see the unseen. A dreamer pushes the edge of the envelope, daring to accomplish something for God's kingdom.

The world has always been changed by the person who embraced a dream and who packed within his own soul the fires to shape it into life.

Walt Disney's mind brought us Mickey Mouse, Minnie, Pluto, and Donald Duck featured in cartoons, films, books, and an endless stream of other memorabilia. But his greatest dream was the transformation of worthless Florida swampland near the city of Orlando into an enchanting world of motels, hotels, resorts, restaurants, rides, and exhibits known as Disneyworld. He died before its completion. An admirer remarked, "Too bad Walt didn't see this before he died." An associate replied, "Oh, but he did."

Martin Luther King, Jr., had a dream. His dream was of peace, brotherhood, and freedom. He said in his famous speech, "I have a dream that my four children will one day live in a nation where they will not be judged by the color of their skin but by the content of their character." His vision was not a lofty ideal but a vivid glance into the future.

The proverb says, "Where there is no vision, the people are unrestrained" (Prov. 29:18 NASB). Like an unbridled horse, leaders without a dream are purposeless. Their energy is wasted on less important things. Priorities are misplaced because there is no direction and focus.

✳Ministry on the cutting edge demands that one begin with the end in mind. In other words, men and women of vision start with a clear understanding of their destination. They know where they are going and the steps to take in order to reach their goal.

When we fail to see the destination, it is easy to get caught up in the activity trap. We work harder; we are busy. But as one man said, "I reached the top of the ladder only to discover it was leaning against the wrong wall." You see, the possibility exists to be busy without being effective. We become like the airplane pilot flying across the Pacific who radioed back to his base, "I don't know where I am going but I'm making great time."

The effectiveness of a ministry requires that its leader

knows what God wants and moves in tandem with Him toward that dream. Those leaders who are making an impact are those who are committed to the completion and fulfillment of their God-ordained dream.

A CESSATION OF SPIRITUAL POWER

Power comes when we tap all the resources that God has made available to us. Spiritual power that makes a difference in the world is drawn from a daily walk with God. We must recognize that God has gifted us and designed us with an energy that will change lives and impact the world.

But spiritual power is easy to lose. An Old Testament story tells of a young man in a seminary that did lose his power. The principal of the school was the prophet Elijah. Enrollment was so healthy that a new dormitory was needed. All the students offered their help in the effort.

One young man borrowed an ax (a very precious implement in those days) and began cutting trees to clear a plot of land by the river for the new building. He began his task with great enthusiasm. But suddenly the ax head flew off the handle and fell into the river. He lost his cutting edge!

"Oh, sir," he cried to Elijah, "it was borrowed." Elijah took a stick and threw it in the water, and the ax head floated to the top.

You don't have to look very far beneath the surface of that event for the spiritual truth to come floating to the top also. It's a sad fact that many leaders are laboring for the Lord and are terribly frustrated because they just don't have the power that is needed to make a sharp impact on this world. They have become dull and lifeless, largely ineffective as change agents in the world.

Vance Havner, writing in reference to the ax head story in 2 Kings, said in his book *The Secret of Christian Joy*, "Many of the Lord's workmen today have lost the ax head of power. They have lost the joy of salvation, they have not the upholding of God's Spirit. The lost ax head of the Spirit's unction has fallen into the waters of worldliness, ponds of indifference, swamps of sluggishness. They have ability, training, sincerity, earnestness, but they are chopping with the handle. They stand before a demonized world powerless, and it must be said of them, as it was said of the disciples before the demon-possessed boy, 'And they could not . . .' (Mark 9:18). The pitiful tragedy of the lost ax heads in the churches today!'"[6]

Has the Christian community grown powerless? We have lost the cutting edge if we are relying on our own ingenuity instead of God's power. Are we depending on man-made programs and activities to the point that we have replaced the power of God in our lives? Programs alone are nothing more than artificial replacements for the Spirit of God working in our lives and churches. Tragically many of us live unaware that God's power is absent. The calendar and schedules are full, but the character is stained and the spirit empty.

Jack Taylor described many modern self-sufficient leaders with the poignant words, "To a large extent, we are going around beating on trees with bare ax handles. At intervals, under the suspicion that this is not getting the job done, we call for strategy conferences on how to make our ax handles more effective or how to improve our swing. We take a census of the trees, motivate the woodchoppers, declare that this is the day for felling forests, and, with polished ax handles and persuasive personnel, we embark toward the woods.

"But alas, though the noise of the workmen is great the sound of falling trees is missing. There is movement without might, energy expended without effectiveness, much doing but little dynamic! There is little to show after all is done but bruised hands, tired bodies, and wounded trees. What is missing? Why, the ax head, of course—the cutting edge of it all. But what is the 'ax head' of the Church? It is the life of God in Christ released in our world through the work of the Holy Spirit! Our bodies, the larger body, the church, with all our abilities and programs are but the handles upon which swings the ax head of His life."[7]

The early disciples ministered on the cutting edge because they were infused with God's power. The world leaders observed the confidence of Peter and John, and understood that they were uneducated and untrained men. What caused this impact? Luke records, "'By what power, or in what name, have you done this?'

"Then Peter, filled with the Holy Spirit, said to them,

'Rulers and elders of the people, if we are on trial today for a benefit done to a sick man, as to how this man has been made well, let it be known to all of you, and to all the people of Israel, that by the name of Jesus Christ the Nazarene, whom you crucified, whom God raised from the dead—by this name this man stands here before you in good health'" (Acts 4:7–10 NASB).

If the power of the Holy Spirit suddenly vacated our lives would things change drastically?

I vividly remember my first commercial airline flight. I traveled from Nashville to Phoenix. A change of planes was made in Dallas. The weather in Dallas was dreary and overcast. The plane ascended out of Dallas into the gray, murky clouds. As I looked out the window I only saw slush in the skies. But suddenly, rather miraculously, the plane burst through the clouds. The sun shone brilliantly. The top side of the clouds sparkled with a white fluff and softness. The sky reflected a deep turquoise of blue. It was an unforgettable experience—a serendipitous moment.

As I look back on that spectacle, I see a stunning parallel to my ministry. For the most part I was ministering beneath the clouds. I was not experiencing the joy, the freedom, the effectiveness, or the power that had been made available to me. I wanted to break through the bonds that were holding me back. I wanted to live each aspect of my life on the cutting edge. I no longer was content to settle for business as usual. I wanted the resources and abundance of God infused in my ministry.

As I have grappled with the issue of effectiveness and as I have studied the effectiveness of others, I have walked away with a conclusion. Those leaders making an impact are perfecting a few God-ordained inner disciplines that not only test their ministry but also make their ministry. People who make a difference—sometimes in highly visible ways, sometimes in quiet ways that are easily overlooked—possess undeniable inner qualities. These qualities, or inner disciplines as I call them, provide the difference of being in the middle of action from watching on the sidelines. They are the keys to effective ministry.

I suspect by the fact that you are reading this book you have a desire to make a difference. But remember that making a difference will not come easy. If it were easy you would have already done it. Making an impact, being effective, requires that you be willing to change, to risk, to dream, and to draw upon God's power. The following pages will unfold for you the inner disciplines that will assist you in making that difference.

Let me remind you that these qualities are hidden. For the most part they are secret. They are only known by you and your God. They don't usually cry for attention. They reside dormant in the inner domain of your private sanctums. They will remain there until called upon. But when they are developed and used they will provide the source of strength for you to produce the changes, risks, dreams, and power that will make your ministry effective. They are like an oil well waiting to be tapped. Or a mother lode of gold waiting to be mined. They are waiting to be brought to the light to assist you in ministering on the cutting edge.

ENDNOTES

1. Michael J. Kami, *Trigger Points* (New York: MacGraw Hill, 1988), 120.

2. George Barna, *The Frog In The Kettle* (Ventura, Calif.: Regal Books, 1990), 21.

3. Karl Marx, quoted in Robert Coleman, *The Master Plan of Evangelism* (Old Tappan, N.J.: Spire Books, 1963), 9.

4. Paul W. Powell, *Go-Givers in a Go-Getter World* (Nashville: Broadman Press, 1986), 11.

5. Ibid., 12.

6. Vance Havner, *The Secret of Christian Joy* (Philadelphia: Pinebrook Book Club, 1938), 58–59.

7. Jack R. Taylor, *Much More* (Nashville: Broadman Press, 1972), 16–17.

2

Vision—How to Make a Lasting Impact

Having spent some time in Europe, I longed to return to the States. The comfort and convenience of home were very appealing. I yearned for a steak on the grill, my own car, directional signs that were written in English, and television. While these American conveniences were lacking, one American product was clearly evident—Coca-Cola.

Robert Woodruff is to blame. You see, Woodruff, while president of Coca-Cola from 1923 to 1955, had the audacity to state during World War II, "We will see that every man in uniform gets a bottle of Coca-Cola for five cents wherever he is and whatever it costs."[1] When the war ended, he went on to say that in his lifetime he wanted everyone in the world to have a taste of Coca-Cola. Talk about vision!

With careful planning and a lot of persistence, Woodruff and his colleagues reached their generation around the globe for Coca-Cola.

How big is your vision and your impact for God's kingdom? Have you ever thought about what God could do through you to influence your generation? Just as Jesus called his disciples to gain a vision for impacting the world, he calls us to do the same.

What exactly is vision? It has been defined in many different ways. Webster defines it as an act of power to see something unseen. Vision is seeing with our minds'-eye that which is not yet seen so that the unseen can become reality. It comprises an ability to see through God's eyes what he wants accomplished through our lives and ministries. It embodies the driving force behind the activity of a true servant of God. It is like a rope that helps us cross a moving river.

In a few simple words allow me to stir your thoughts on how you can impact this world for Christ through a powerful vision.

CURIOSITY

In every person who truly makes a difference in this world is the characteristic of curiosity. Curiosity is where dreams are born. Curiosity seeks an answer to the question, What if? Thomas Edison asked, what if? and now we don't sit around in the dark. Roger Bannister asked, "What if I trained and worked harder than anyone else, could the four-minute-mile be broken?" He did and it was.

In the Christian realm, Millard Fuller wondered about building houses for poor people who could not otherwise own homes of their own. Fuller organized Habitat for Humanity which now provides homes in over 450 communities across the United States and around the world. Each day as many as six houses are completed and offered to poor families at only the cost of construction. Materials are often donated and volunteers do the construction work. No down payment is required, and the long-term mortgages provided involve no interest payments. The price of these housing units is incredibly low.

Another person who asked the question, what if? was Charles Colson. The former chief counsel for Richard Nixon was indicted in the Watergate cover-up. He became a Christian during this experience. While in prison he discovered an unmet need. He encountered men and women who had been ignored by the church, pushed around by society, and often forsaken by family and friends. Prison became a place of revelation and calling. He made a decision to do something about all of this, and upon release he founded Prison Fellowship. This program gets ordinary Christians to do what they can to express love and concern for those behind bars in their local communities.

Others have asked, what if? and in less dramatic ways have made a solid difference in the world. Children's homes have been built, care for unwed mothers has been initiated, ministries to single adults, business leaders, mothers of preschoolers, and more have begun because a few people have asked, what if?

Have you ever asked the question of yourself, What if? What if I used my talent for God's glory? What if I gave of my time in an extraordinary way to an unmet need in my community? What if I invested my gifts to the cause for which I'm deeply concerned? What if I got busy and got involved?

We need to ask, What if? often. What if we were bold in asking God to do something great through us? What if we trusted God completely for a grand happening? What if we were completely sold out to making a difference for Christ in our community? What if we rallied together to accomplish some great task for God's kingdom?

⋇What if? is a very important question. Curiosity is a distinctive mark of one making an impact for God's kingdom. But other traits are needed.

COURAGE

Nothing in life was ever achieved without courage. That's why throughout Scripture God instructs us, "Be courageous." Courage is not the absence of fear, but the ability to walk on in spite of it. Winston Churchill, who knew something about courage, said, "Success is never final; failure is never fatal; it is the courage to continue that counts."

It is easy to stay in ruts. It is easy not to make a dent on this world when one chooses complacency and inactivity. The truth is that I have never lost a race for political office, I have never been defeated in a marathon race, I have never choked up while singing a solo. That's because I've never tried any of those things. Only people who try run the risk of failure. But only those who attempt things achieve success. Charles Kettering said, "You will never stub your toe ⋇ standing still. The faster you go, the more chance there is of stubbing your toe, but the more chance you have of getting somewhere."[2]

We have been deceived into this complacent attitude that says, Take care, or Take it easy, when the Biblical attitude is, Take courage and go for it.

Recently I came across an interesting story about a writer. He writes, "When I was a young writer with a very uncertain income, I went into a quiet park to contemplate a serious problem. For four years I had been engaged but didn't dare to marry. There was no way of foreseeing how little I might earn in the next year; moreover, we had long cherished a plan of living and writing in Paris, Rome, Vienna, London—everywhere. But how could we go three thousand miles away from everything that was familiar and secure, without the certainty of some money now and then?

At that moment I looked up and saw a squirrel jump from one high tree to another. He appeared to be aiming for a limb so far out of reach that the leap looked like suicide. He missed—but landed, safe and unconcerned, on a branch several feet lower. Then he climbed to his goal, and all was well. An old man sitting on the bench said, 'Funny, I've seen hundreds of 'em jump like that, especially when there are dogs around and they can't come down to the ground. A lot of 'em miss, but I've never seen any hurt in trying.' Then he chuckled. 'I guess they've got to risk it if they don't want to spend their lives in one tree.' I thought, 'A squirrel takes a chance—have I less nerve than a squirrel?' We were married in two weeks, scraped up enough money for our passage and sailed across the Atlantic—jumping off into space, not sure what branch we'd land on. I began to write twice as fast and twice as hard as ever before. And to our amazement we promptly soared into the realm of respectable incomes. Since then, whenever I have to choose between risking a new venture or hanging back, those five little words run through my thoughts: 'Once there was a squirrel . . . .' And sometimes I hear the old man on the park bench saying, 'They've got to risk it if they don't want to spend their lives in one tree.'"[3]

I think of all those people of the likes of William Carey, who have risked their lives and jumped by faith to make a difference in this world for Christ. Carey, the father of the modern missions movement, left the comfort of his cobbler's bench to travel to India to carry the cause of Christ. Or a modern-day Carey, David Wilkerson, who left the comfort of a respectable pastorate in Pennsylvania to go to the inner city of New York to work with the gangs and drug addicts to lead them to Christ.

These are men of courage. They risked their lives for the cause of Christ.

COMPASSION

To make an impact for God on this world means seeing people as objects of God's love. As Jesus and his disciples walked the dusty roads of Palestine, Jesus saw individuals, while the disciples saw only the masses. The disciples saw people who were hurting, and they wanted to run, while Jesus saw people in need and wanted to help. In other words, Jesus saw people who were lost and helpless and his heart broke.

Bob Pierce began World Vision, a hunger relief organization, because in his travels around the world he saw individuals who were hungry and cold and in need of assistance. These were precious individuals for whom Christ had died. Pierce's lifelong motto became "May my heart be broken with the things that break the heart of God."

Most of us look at a suffering world, and even at the poor, the sick, and the old in our own communities, and think "That's awful! But what could I do?" The problems loom so large and complicated that we feel helpless and do nothing. Eventually we grow immune.

A tiny Yugoslavian nun has answered that, What can one person do? dilemma for herself once and for all. Every day for the past thirty years, Mother Teresa and her followers have cheerfully lived and worked in the world's worst slum, trying to share God's love and care with the hopeless people of Calcutta's streets.

Ironically, Mother Teresa's selfless service and compassion have made her one of the best-loved and most respected women in the world. She is recognized wherever she goes. Kings, presidents, and popes have honored her with awards, medals, and degrees. Everywhere her name is synonymous with Christian charity and service. Her compassion has made a profound difference in this world.

⚹A warning is in order, however. Compassion is costly. It is much easier to stay in the comfort of our Christian fellowship than it is to reach out to others in need. But the longer we stay in that comfortable cocoon, the more our compassion for those who are outside of a relationship with Christ diminishes.

While curiosity causes us to ask the right questions, compassion causes us to look in the right direction. We begin to see people from God's perspective. We begin to identify needs. We start to understand how we can make a difference for Christ.

COMMISSION

Jesus not only wanted his disciples to have a love for the lost, but also to lead the lost to salvation. He not only wanted us to recognize needs, he also wanted us to begin the process of meeting those needs. God has never been casual about the lost. And he has given us the responsibility to carry the good news to those people.

It was the heartfelt vision to reach the unreached that sent Dr. John Geddie, a Canadian Presbyterian missionary, to the New Hebrides Islands in the South Pacific. He was in constant peril of his life but won the confidence of the dangerous cannibals. He developed an alphabet and translated the New Testament into their dialect. One by one he taught them, and they gave up their heathen gods and superstitions. Today a stone tablet bears testimony of Geddie's vision for these unreached people and his faithfulness for twenty-four years of service. Its inscription is a challenge to us today:

When he landed in 1848, there were no Christians.
When he left in 1872, there were no heathen.

Geddie had a vision, a dream, and he gave his life to the fulfillment of it. Just one man. One man whose life bore the mark of the eternal invading the temporal. He took Christ's words to heart and made an impact on his world for Christ.

For three weeks I studied with pastors from Eastern Europe. They were men who did not have the many modern tools and resources that clergy in the United States have available to them. But these men are making inroads for the gospel to hearts that were once closed and cut off by communism. They don't talk about the petty things that infiltrate the American church scene. They are taking the gospel to the streets. They are proactive in reaching their world for Christ. And they are making a difference.

I once heard a preacher say: "Millions will die today and go to hell and most of you don't give a damn. (Pause.) The sad thing is that most of you are more disturbed that I used the word 'damn' than the fact millions are dying and going to hell without Christ."

Our generation is responsible for spreading the gospel to our generation. Each church is responsible for communicating the good news to its community. We are not responsible for the response, but we are responsible for sharing. The task is ours.

Jesus always sent out the workers. Many projects and jobs exist within the church building for us to perform. But by and large our commission is out there. Often, we barricade ourselves within the church fortress. We have heard more sermons on evangelism than we care to recall. We have been through endless evangelism training programs. We have been edified and equipped and endowed. But we are negligent in going. Unfortunately, we, as the late Peter Marshall described, "are like deep sea divers, encased in suits designed for many fathoms deep, marching bravely to pull out plugs in bath tubs." We have been prepared and trained to make a great impact but instead we settle for mediocrity and insignificance.

COMMITMENT

The final ingredient in making a lasting impact for God is commitment. Commitment spells the difference from living in the shallows of existence to living in the depths of achievement. Commitment is the ingredient that transforms mediocrity into magnificence. Commitment is what separates dreamers from doers.

John Wesley, the founder of the Methodist church, once stated, "If I had 300 men sold out to God we could set the world on fire." I am convinced that if every pastor had 30 persons sold out to God they could set their community on fire.

Jesus has always sought people who would be committed to him and to his kingdom. He began with twelve. And except for Judas who betrayed him, and John, each disciple died a martyr's death. They were sold out to the cause. Once Jesus spoke to his followers, "The harvest is plentiful but the workers are few" (Matt. 9:37). In other words, there was a great need, but only a few were willing to make a commitment of selling out to God. Times haven't changed much. When one examines the qualifications of those disciples one would have wondered if they could make a dent in society. The disciples were ordinary men. But just as God took stones the builders had rejected to build his kingdom, he took these ordinary men to change the world.

God doesn't need superstars. He needs the likes of you and me—simple people who simply want to do something for God. Ordinary people who want to make a difference. The truth is that Christ can take an ordinary person and use him or her in an extraordinary way to change lives, to change situations, to change the world, if that person is willing to commit himself or herself completely to Christ's will.

There is only one kind of effective Christian—a totally committed Christian. Anything less than total commitment is unacceptable to God. He demands total commitment.

Once you have defined your vision for ministry, go after it. Vision without obedience is defiance to God. When God has directed, it is in our best interest to respond. Remember Jonah?

What would God have you do with your life? How will you make an impact for God's kingdom? Don't be satisfied with anything less than God's best.

ENDNOTES

1. Luis Palau, *Dream Great Dreams* (Portland, Oreg.: Multnomah Press, 1984), 1.

2. Ted W. Engstrom, *The Pursuit of Excellence* (Grand Rapids: Zondervan, 1982), 37–38.

3. James S. Hewett, ed., *Illustrations Unlimited* (Wheaton: Tyndale, 1988), 128–129.

3

Investments—
Sharpening One's Life

Two lumberjacks, a young one and an older one, raced to see who could cut down the most trees in a single day. When the day was completed the winner was obvious. The older lumberjack had won hands down. The younger lumberjack could not believe it. "How could you cut down more trees than I did? Every hour I saw you sitting down, while I kept right on cutting. I don't understand."

"Truly, you don't," said the older man.

"How could you have cut more trees by sitting so much?"

"That's because when I sat down I was sharpening my saw. Why didn't you stop to sharpen your saw?"

"I didn't have time to sharpen the saw," the younger man said emphatically. "I was too busy sawing!"

One of the most powerful investments I can make in life is a personal investment—my mental, physical, social, and spiritual well-being. In reality, I am the only instrument I have with which to deal with life and to contribute to it. To be effective, to make my life count, I need to recognize the importance of taking time regularly to sharpen the saw of my life.

Sharpening the saw is not just a good idea, it is a biblical principle.*"A dull ax requires great strength; be wise and sharpen the blade" (Eccl. 10:10 LB). The task before me is not to work harder, but smarter. It takes more than strength of body, dedication to a project, or mental acumen to bring success in an endeavor. Also, I need the wisdom to understand God's timing and my need to personally replenish and rejuvenate my soul so I will be ready when called upon. I have come to realize that I never waste time when I sharpen the saw.

Jesus provides the perfect example.*He was busy but never in a hurry. He lived in the midst of a constant storm, but he was always at peace.*He was pressed to the limits of emotional and spiritual involvement, but he was never stressed out. What was his secret?

Jesus, even though he was God's Son, knew the value of sharpening the saw. A quick study of Jesus' life reveals that *he did not make himself available to everyone. In fact, there were times when he got away from the masses. He cherished his time alone. He needed that time for replenishment and refreshment. In essence, he was sharpening his saw.

If Jesus needed time alone for personal rejuvenation, so do I. I have learned that I need to do the following.

TAKE TIME TO REST

Most of the time I live life at full throttle, which leads to exhaustion. I become sick and tired of being sick and tired.

Stress and burnout are not only symptoms of our day, for many they have become a way of life. It is most unfortunate that we deplore drug and alcohol addicts but somehow promote and admire the work addict. William McNamara, author of *The Human Adventure*, has said, "Possibly the greatest malaise in our country today is our neurotic compulsion to work." This stressed-out feeling has invaded our churches too. Tim Hansel observed in his book *When I Relax I Feel Guilty* that dedicated Christians too often are characterized by frantic activity, fatigue, and weariness, rather than love, compassion, and joy.[1] *

A restless lifestyle produces a life filled with stress and worry. One becomes a prime candidate for burnout. Rest and relaxation are not optional. In fact, rest is so important that God included it in the Ten Commandments. The

Sabbath was made for man because God knows that our physical, emotional, and spiritual well-being demands periodic breaks. The old proverb is true, "If you don't come apart and rest awhile, you will come apart."

As a pastor, I have come to realize that my job is never finished. I simply can't say I'll get some rest when I finish the work or have the time. That time never comes. I have to make the time to rest. [Rest was never meant to be a luxury, but rather a necessity for those who want to grow and mature.]

Brother Jeremiah, a monk, reflected on his many years of Christian service. He'd worked hard, sometimes too hard. He'd taken life seriously. As he approached the end of his active service to others, he sat down and wrote these words:

"If I had my life to live over again, I'd try to make more mistakes next time. I would relax. I would limber up. I would be sillier than I have been this trip. I know of very few things I would take seriously. I would take more trips. I would climb more mountains, swim more rivers, and watch more sunsets. I would do more walking and looking.

"If I had my life to live over, I would start barefooted earlier in the spring and stay that way later in the fall. I would play more. I would ride on more merry-go-rounds. I'd pick more daisies."

I was encouraged early in my ministry by my senior pastor to take time off. My first week on the job he emphasized, "Thursday is your day off. I don't want to see your face around this office or this church. Stay home, relax, read, play, but don't come here. You may not understand my point now but someday you will thank me for this." He was right. And I do thank him for reinforcing what I need to sustain energy for effective results.

DEEPEN MY RELATIONSHIP WITH CHRIST

Jesus always took time for his relationship with his Father. The Scriptures reveal, "Very early in the morning, while it was still dark, Jesus got up, left the house and went off to a solitary place, where he prayed" (Mark 1:35). No matter how busy Jesus was he made a practice of spending time alone with God. If Jesus made time for deepening his relationship with God when he was busy, how much more do you and I need it?

There are three phases to this relationship:

Come. The relationship has to be entered. It requires a step of faith. In coming, Jesus invites us to take his hand.

Commitment. Once the relationship has been established, a commitment must be made. We now walk with Jesus. At this phase, many people fall short in the relationship. They come to Christ but they fail to walk with Christ. A relationship with Christ is more than taking a step of faith, it necessitates walking in a life of obedience.

Communication. On the heels of the commitment phase is the need to communicate with one another. We must talk with Christ. Dialogue. Get to know one another. Imperative to this relationship, as with any other, is the fact that a relationship is never achieved with a single encounter; it develops as two people grow in their knowledge of one another over time.

When I was a junior in college, a religion major studying for the ministry, a cold sweat came over me along with a distressing thought: "Could it be that I don't know God?" The thought was wreaking havoc on my mind. I had grown up in the church. My parents had a vibrant faith. But I felt empty and alone. The person of Jesus Christ, whom I was telling others about, was distant. Perhaps I didn't know him at all.

I grew up next door to the church. I went to church every time the doors where open, and many times when they weren't. I was faithful to Vacation Bible School, youth activities, revivals, and every other event at church. I could quote Bible verses, I knew all the books of the Bible, I even made speeches and gave testimonies at church. I volunteered for lifelong Christian service. But now something was missing. My faith was weak and depleted.

A friend challenged me to read through the Gospels while asking God, "If you are really who you say that you are, would you reveal yourself to me?" In a matter of months, I discovered once again who God was. And he was very real. I came to know God in a deeper and more intimate way. I discovered that I simply had not allowed the relationship to deepen.

I had come to Christ. But I had allowed religious activities to replace the needed communication with him. As I returned to my quiet place and my quiet time the freshness of God's presence permeated my life. My relationship was strengthened.

Spiritually we can't function without deepening our relationship with Christ. Without this time of communing with God we will wither spiritually as well as lose our effectiveness in ministry. The psalmist said, "Come, let us bow down in worship, let us kneel before the LORD our Maker" (Psalm 95:6). Deepening our relationship with God gets us in touch with our Creator. It keeps us in tune with our Redeemer. It reminds us again and again of how little we are and how great God is. On another occasion, the psalmist wrote, "Be still, and know that I am God" (Psalm 46:10). We live in a polluted world. But the pollution that affects us as leaders is noise, hurry, and crowds. If Satan can keep us busy and engaged in much activity, listening to other voices besides God's, he will rest satisfied. Consequently, we will lose our sharp edge.

Spending time with God is to the Christian what the mainspring is to a watch, what the engine is to a car. It is the very core, the essential element. Without worship we dry up and die. Why? Simply because we lose contact with the source of our spiritual life. An old miner once explained to a visitor, "I let my mules spend one day a week outside the mines to keep them from going blind." The Christian leader who does not spend time each day away from the daily grind of life deepening his or her relationship with God goes blind in the soul. As we daily spend time in prayer and in his Word our relationship with God will be deepened and our ministry effectiveness will be broadened.

DEVELOP THE HABIT OF LIFELONG LEARNING

Jesus made the commitment to lifelong learning. "And Jesus grew in wisdom and stature, and in favor with God and men" (Luke 2:52). Jesus not only grew physically, spiritually, and socially, he grew mentally. Jesus was a student. He was a student of nature, relationships, current events, geography, civic affairs, and more. He listened, he observed, he asked questions, he pondered. He called his followers to be students as well. A process of lifelong learning is needed.

One of the great tragedies of our society is that many people stop learning when they finish school. They no longer study or write or read. The attraction of the easier avenues of entertainment (such as television) and the busy pace of life distract us from growing intellectually. The Christian who is not growing intellectually is like a book whose many pages remain unopened and unread. In fact, one Christian book editor commented that "for every ten books purchased, only one is read." This is a frightening indication of stagnant minds. Stagnant minds are lifeless minds, like a stagnant pond—germ-infested, dirty, and a disgrace.

The mind is truly a terrible thing to waste. The challenges that lay before the Christian community today can only be confronted by people who are on the cutting edge of learning. The writer of Proverbs said, "Wisdom is supreme; therefore get wisdom. Though it cost all you have, get understanding" (Prov. 4:7). The best investment one can make is in education, both formal and informal. As a former president of Harvard University once remarked, "If you think education is expensive, try ignorance."

John Wesley once received a note that said: "The Lord has told me to tell you that he doesn't need your book-learning, your Greek and your Hebrew."

Wesley answered, "Thank you, sir. Your letter was superfluous, however, as I already knew the Lord has no need for my 'book-learning,' as you put it. However, although the Lord has not directed me to say so, on my own responsibility I would like to say to you that the Lord does not need your ignorance either."

Why should we invest the time and energy into a pursuit of lifelong learning? The reason is simple. The goal of learning is not information but life transformation. John Milton wrote, "The end of learning is to know God, and out of that knowledge to love him, and to imitate him." As we learn we grow in the things of God. We become more and more like him. We become better equipped to face the challenges of each day and we develop the potential for growth in our ministries. Growing ministries require growing ministers—men and women committed to a lifelong pursuit of learning.

It is worth noting the words of the eighteenth-century poet Edward Young, "Learning makes a man fit company for himself." I might add that it makes one a fit leader of others, as well.

REFLECT ON MY LIFE

For the saw to remain sharp, we must consistently commit ourselves to a personal checkup. Just as a government needs a system of checks and balances so does an effective, productive life. People on the cutting edge reflect on their life often.

A few years ago, three dedicated Christian businessmen in my church lost their jobs. After several weeks of job searching they came to me individually to talk. Interestingly, each wanted to know what I thought about him leaving the business sector of life and returning to seminary to pursue a life in the ministry. As each laid out their ideas, the questions that raced through my mind were: "Why are you considering such an alternative? Why are you thinking of this at this time in your life? What caused you to consider such a career change?" One common thread ran through each man's story. Each man prefaced his remarks by saying, "You know, I've been doing a lot of serious thinking lately."

These were fine Christian laymen. Eventually they found jobs and none enrolled in seminary. But by their own admission their eyes had been closed to what their careers had meant to them. It took the loss of a job for them to reflect on their lives.

I suggest that people who want to stay on the cutting edge must reflect on their lives each week. And as a part of that reflection they should ask three questions of themselves.

The first question is: Where is God in my life? God should be in the center of our lives—work, family, recreation, church, and school. It is easy for our lives to get out of balance, causing God to slide off center. Each week we should take the time to see where God is and to request that he return to the center of our lives.

The second question we need to ask is: What is really

important? We should examine our busy lives, especially our work. Many people climb the ladder of success only to discover what they sought was not really important, at least by eternity's standards. On his or her deathbed no one says, I wish I had spent more time with my business. When people gather around your grave what will they say about you? They will talk. And what they talk about will be what was really important in your life.

The third question we need to ask is: Where am I going? In answer to this question we determine to pursue Christ-centered goals. We ponder where we are headed in the coming week, month, and year. We define our intentions and make our dedications. Sadly, many Christians do not know where they are going. They are aimless and purposeless. The philosopher Santayana told us, "A fanatic is one who, having lost sight of his aim, redoubles his effort."[2] Much of the haste and worry in this world is because people have failed to reflect on where they are going.

How sharp is your life?

Billy Graham once said that if he had the last ten years of his life to live over, he would withdraw more often for times of rest, meditation on the Word, and prayer so he could give himself completely to the battle when he needed to.

When we take sufficient time to rest and worship and learn and reflect, the Lord renews, gives insight, and energizes us to accomplish twice as much when we jump back into the job at hand.

ENDNOTES

1. Tim Hansel, *When I Relax I Feel Guilty* (Elgin, Ill.: Life Journey Books, 1979), 34.

2. Geroge Sontayona, quoted in E. Paul Hovey, *The Treasury of Inspirational Anecdotes, Quotations, and Illustrations* (Grand Rapids: Revell, 1959), 179.

4

Balance—*Maintaining Stability in a Seesaw World*

You've probably witnessed those people who frantically keep ten or so plates spinning on poles. Hurriedly they scurry from one plate to another rousing to life any that are losing momentum. It becomes exhausting just watching these people try to control the chaos.

Have you ever felt this way? I have.

Some time ago, I realized something was distorted in my personal life. I was irritable and easily ticked off. I loathed getting out of bed in the mornings. The joy of serving God had departed me. At times, I broke down sobbing. I entertained thoughts of leaving God's work. Something was wrong. I knew it.

After several months of trying to figure out my problem, the diagnosis was revealed to me at a conference. The conference focused on the pastor's personal life. The leaders had experienced similar frustrations as mine. The conference was truly a life-changing event for me. I came back with several conclusions.

First, I love ministry. But, as I reflected on my downward spiral, I saw I was devoting too much emotional and physical energy to the task. Spiritually and emotionally I was depleted. I was not tired *of* the work of God, but I was definitely tired *in* the work of God. My love for the ministry had become an addiction. It was not enough to serve a church, I wanted a big church. I became engrossed in numbers and dollars and statistics. I had lost sight of my passion for helping and serving others.

Second, I desired to stay in the ministry for the long haul. I didn't want to be another statistic of one who did not finish, another ministerial fatality strewn on the highway of burnout. I knew of too many capable and gifted ministers who did not fulfill their calling. I did not want to be listed among their ranks.

Third, I would not sacrifice my family on the altar of ministry. How easy it becomes to neglect one's family at the expense of God's work. (A minister who loses his family loses it all.) As much as I was committed to staying in the ministry, I determined that I would rather leave the ministry than lose my family.

Can you identify with what I am talking about? Maybe you are struggling with similar concerns. All some people have to do is substitute job, or success, or friends, or hobby where I have used the word ministry. Overemphasizing one area of life causes life to carom out of control.

If you are struggling with similar issues, what you and I need to learn is balance.

THE MEANING OF BALANCE

Defining a balanced life is not easy. A balanced life is characterized by order, peace, and wholeness. The various parts of this life are as they should be and where they should be. Each part of the balanced life gets the right amount of time and effort at the right time. It's not giving each part of life the same amount of time that makes life balanced; it's giving each part the necessary allotment of time.

We can compare living a balanced life to eating a balanced diet. Such a diet would have the correct amounts, not equal amounts, of the basic food groups necessary for proper health.

THE MODELING OF BALANCE

Perhaps it would be easier to comprehend a balanced life if one could visualize such a life. An Old Testament character who modeled balance was Daniel. The Scriptures say of Daniel, "Now Daniel so distinguished himself among the administrators and the satraps by his exceptional qualities that the king planned to set him over the whole kingdom" (Dan. 6:3). What was it that distinguished Daniel's life? Of the many gifts he possessed he was able to demonstrate balance.

Daniel had been taken captive and deported to Babylon by Nebuchadnezzar in 605 B.C. He was not selected by accident. He was chosen for his outstanding qualities. "Bring in some of the Israelites from the royal family and the nobility—young men without any physical defect, handsome, showing aptitude for every kind of learning, well informed, quick to understand, and qualified to serve in the king's palace. . . . Daniel resolved not to defile himself. . . . Daniel so distinguished himself among the administrators and the satraps by his exceptional qualities that the king planned to set him over the whole kingdom" (Dan. 1:3–4, 8; 6:3). From this brief description of Daniel's life, I discover six areas in which he excelled. These provide a framework for the areas we are to keep in balance.

① *The physical dimension.* This would entail exercise, proper rest, and sufficient nourishment.

② *The mental dimension.* This area encompasses learning and studying.

③ *The relational dimension.* Our relationships need to be fine-tuned and balanced.

④ *The spiritual dimension.* Often in one's effort to make the most out of life, one neglects God's role in one's life.

⑤ *The vocational dimension.* This is the one area that often throws the other dimensions out of balance. Most of us have to work to provide for our families, but it must always be kept in proper relation to the other dimensions.

⑥ *The family dimension.* Closely related to the relational dimension, room in one's life must be provided for one's family.

These dimensions would best be displayed in a pie shape, not a list. When we list priorities we often major on the top two or three and neglect the bottom few. When listing the dimensions as a pie another warning is in order. Each sector should not be drawn with equal portions, but with the correct and proper portion allotted to keep all of life in balance. For example, if one tried to divide the pie in accordance to time constraints there wouldn't be enough time for all six if work comprises eight hours per day.

As you examine the basic components of your life, how do you measure up? Is each area balanced? Is each area getting the proper amount of time? Do you find that you are overemphasizing one? Do you discover that you have neglected an essential area?

THE MASTERING OF BALANCE

Since life is made up of many parts, each demanding our time and energy, balance is needed to bring order to the parts, thereby strengthening the whole of life.

Achieving balance is finding the controlling center of life. In order to balance a yard stick on your finger, for example, you must find the center. The same is true with our lives. This controlling center masters us, we don't master it.

If someone's career, for example, is the controlling center, then that career determines what books to read, seminars to attend, people to network, and decisions to make. In such a scenario, one does not master one's career, one's career masters one. The same is true for money, success, goals, status, or whatever else may be the controlling center.

Two key events in Daniel's life will bring light on his controlling center. "Daniel resolved not to defile himself with the royal food and wine" (Dan. 1:8). And "Three times a day he got down on his knees and prayed, giving thanks to his God, just as he had done before" (Dan. 6:10). Whether it had to do with his physical intake of food or his spiritual intake of prayer, the most important thing in his life was his relationship with God. While he could have easily justified a neglect in this area, being miles away from home and in a foreign land, he remained true to his controlling center— his relationship with God.

I realize that during my depression my church was mastering me. Every aspect of my life was viewed in light of my church's growth. Consequently, my church was destroying my life. What I needed was what I preached: Christ at the center of my life. I had to relearn that life is balanced when I put God in his proper place. When I concentrate on Jesus being the controlling center, I find everything else taking its proper place. To bring order and balance back to my life was to invite Christ's control over every segment of my life. How sad, what I had proclaimed from the pulpit, I had mistakenly failed to apply to my own life.

Thomas Kelly wrote in *A Testament of Devotion* about the importance of having Christ at the center of our lives. "We are trying to be several selves at once, without all our selves being organized by a single, mastering Life within us." He adds, "Life is meant to be lived from a Center, a divine Center. Each one of us can live such a life of amazing power and peace and serenity of integration and confidence and simplified multiplicity, on one condition—that is, *if we really want to.*"[1]

In order for Christ to remain at the center, I must ask myself, How does this event or decision relate to Jesus being the controlling center of my life? Will this choice create control or chaos in my life? Will this consequence cause an equilibrium in my life or will it throw me off balance?

When Christ is in his proper place my life is balanced. Without him my life becomes distorted and out of control.

THE MAINTAINING OF BALANCE

A spider built his web in a barn, high up among the rafters, where he started by spinning a long, thin thread attached to the end of one of the beams. With this thread still attached to him, the spider jumped off the beam and spun out more thread on the way down, until he reached the place he planned as the center of his web. From the center he then spun out other threads like the spokes of a wheel, attaching each of them to the walls and other places. Finally, he had an exquisitely made web, that helped him catch many fine fat flies. This caused him to grow fat and lazy and vain.

One day he was admiring the web he had spun and he noticed the long fine thread he had first spun from the top beam and said, "I wonder what that is for? I can't imagine why I ever put it there—it doesn't catch any flies." And so on a sudden impulse he broke it. But as a result the whole wonderful web collapsed. The spider had forgotten that the one thread—the link to the strongest beam above—supported the whole web. It is very much the same when we break the supporting link with God.

⚹Once the controlling center of life is in place, it must be constantly guarded. A failure to do so results in breaking the vital link to balance. I soon learned some important principles for maintaining balance.

First, determine to stay balanced. "Daniel *resolved* not to defile himself with royal food and wine" (Dan. 1:8). The word *resolve* means to make up your mind. Personally, I had to make up my mind that if my life would move toward balance it was up to me. That involved a conscious and willful choice to keep God as the controlling center of my life.

This daily decision meant saying no to some better agenda items in order to say yes to the best things. It meant confronting some influential people who would rather I succumb to their unbalanced and uncontrolled way of life.

Not long after I made this decision, I scheduled certain nights with my family. Then, I was asked by a church leader to visit prospective Bible study workers.

"Tim, I would love to make those visits on a Monday or Wednesday night, but I simply can't on Tuesday. That's one of my nights with my family."

"But Rick, this is ministry. I can't understand why you are neglecting this opportunity."

"That's my point. I have neglected my family too long. They require my ministry too."

Tim didn't fully recognize the issue at stake. I hope that in time he will come to realize the magnitude of my decision.

Second, develop a consistent time of prayer. "Three times a day he got down on his knees and prayed, giving thanks to his God, just as he had done before" (Dan. 6:10). To keep Christ at the controlling center demands a consistent contact with him.

Martin Luther, the leader of the Protestant Reformation, said, "I have so much to do today, I'll need to spend another hour on my knees." My typical response to an over committed schedule of daily activities was to say, "I have so much to do today, I'll skip my time with God." Prayer for too long had become a mechanical duty, rather than a source of power in releasing and multiplying God's energies and wisdom.

Through prayer God keeps me focused on him. A focused life is a balanced life. Through prayer I expose my activities to God and allow him to perform the necessary surgery so that my life stays balanced.

For Christ to be the controlling center, prayer must not become a little habit tucked on the periphery of life, it must be my life. I habitually now invest the first moments of the day with my heavenly Father. I allow him to speak to me and direct me. To me, prayer is a symphony and God is the conductor. I give him the freedom to direct my life.

Third, depend on friends for support. "Then Daniel returned to his house and explained the matter to his friends. . . . He urged them to plead for mercy from the God of heaven concerning this mystery" (Dan. 2:17–18). Daniel was in a foreign land separated from family. He was not alone though. He drew strength from his friends.

Never underestimate the power of friends to draw one back to the center. The ancient rabbis used to say, "Anyone who goes too far alone goes mad." The same is true in our spiritual lives. True friends keep us on track and in touch with the stabilizing force of our lives.

Some boys were walking along an abandoned railroad track. They were trying to determine how far they could walk balancing themselves on the tracks. They were not very successful. Then one of the boys got an idea. He yelled out to the leader, "I bet I can walk farther on the tracks than you can." Then reaching over to his friend who was on the adjacent track linking hands they walked farther and longer, perfectly balanced.

That's what friends do for me. Part of my recovery was due to a group of friends that I meet with once a month. These friends have covenanted together to encourage each other to stay on center. They hold me accountable. They ask the tough questions. They offer the faithful wounds of a friend.

I confess that I have not attained a perfectly balanced life. But I have come to realize that I have had to give up some speed in the interest of maintaining my balance. Just as in riding a bicycle down a hill and around a sharp curve in the road, if we fail to maintain our balance certain consequences result. In the last few months I have learned that ultimately the loss of balance is more painful than giving up the speed in life. In order to negotiate the curves and corners of my life, I must continually strive to maintain balance.

Granted, I still struggle in this area of my life, but I am moving in the right direction. I have come to realize that on this side of eternity, God does not expect perfection, only progress.

ENDNOTES

1. Thomas R. Kelly, *A Testament of Devotion* (New York: Harper and Brothers Publishers, 1941), 114, 116.

5

Priorities—*Who's on First?*
What's on Second?

Sometimes I have so many irons in the fire that I feel like I'm putting out the fire. I seek to accomplish so many pursuits. I am bombarded with demands on my time. My schedule becomes a maze of opportunities and deadlines. Instead of getting ahead I feel like I sink further behind.

When I stop to evaluate, I realize that my frustration goes deeper than a shortage of time. My problem, most often, is one of priorities.

Charles Schwab, president of Bethlehem Steel, was approached by a consultant named Ivy Lee about a way to get more work done. Lee offered Schwab a plan that involved (1) writing down the six most important tasks to do the next day, (2) numbering them in order of importance, and then (3) doing them in that order. As an addendum, the fourth step was to realize that any that weren't done could be left till the next day. Lee asked Schwab to use the system for himself. Once he thought it was worthwhile, he could pay Lee whatever he felt it was worth.

A few weeks later Schwab sent Lee a check for $25,000.[1]

The system has become a standard in time management seminars. This system's underlying emphasis on priorities applies not only to daily activities, but also to lifetime pursuits. Without taking charge of our lives, determining what is really important, we will never accomplish what we want, nor make a difference for God and his kingdom. Otherwise, pressures, other people, our own weaknesses, and natural laziness will take over. We will fritter our life away for nothing.

E. M. Gray spent his life searching for the one denominator that all successful people share. He wrote an essay entitled "The Common Denominator of Success." He found that the common denominator of successful people was not hard work, good luck, or astute human relations, although these characteristics were important. The one factor that seemed to transcend all the rest was the habit of putting first things first. He observed, "The successful person has the habit of doing the things failures don't like to do. They don't like doing them either necessarily. But their disliking is subordinated to the strength of their purpose."[2]

We will never live on the cutting edge until we determine who and what comes first. As Dr. Richard C. Halverson has indicated, "Priorities are not just marginal options . . . they are life determining. One's personality is molded inescapably into the image of his priorities."[3] The person living on the cutting edge must select from those options life presents—the ones that will honor Christ.

Deciding what is important is the most difficult decision one will ever make. Those choices don't come quickly nor do they come easily. But in making those tough decisions we usher a great freedom into our lives. We also make future choices easier because we have already made the decision of what we will do. Life becomes more fulfilling and rewarding. Allow me to share with you five reasons why deciding what is important is so important.

AVOID THE URGENT

Deciding what is important will help you to avoid the tyranny of the urgent. You and I live in a constant tension between the urgent and the important. The problem is that the important tasks seldom must be done today or even this week. They don't scream to be accomplished hurriedly. Spending time with God, reading the Bible, praying, visiting a friend, and making quality time for your spouse can all wait. But urgent tasks, the unopened mail, the telephone ringing, the unplanned interruption, call for action, now. Former president Dwight D. Eisenhower said, "The urgent is seldom important, and the important is seldom urgent."[4] Yet too often we allow the tyranny of the urgent to dictate and control our lives.

Several years ago when I was just starting out in the ministry a trusted senior pastor gave me some wise advice. At the time, little did I realize the impact his words would make and how abundantly true they were. He said, "Rick, never, never allow the urgent to take precedent over the important in your life." Years later I am still reminded of the powerful wisdom in that statement. Each day the demands and pressures and emergencies of this world seek to crowd out what is really important.

How do we keep from becoming slaves to the tyranny of the urgent? The answer is found in the life of Jesus. In his prayer in John 17 he makes an interesting, if not startling statement, "I have brought you glory on earth by completing the work you gave me to do" (John 17:4). Did that mean that Jesus had healed everyone? Did that mean that all had received forgiveness? Were all human needs met? No. But he had finished the purpose for which he had come. His life was not devoid of pressures and emergencies and frustrations. Yet he could separate between the urgent and the important. How? Because he knew his purpose, his priority, his mission in coming to this earth.

On one occasion Jesus received a message, "Lord, the one you love is sick" (John 11:3). What could be more urgent than to receive word that your closest friend was dying? "Yet," John says, "when he heard that Lazarus was sick, he stayed where he was two more days" (John 11:6). What was the urgent need? Obviously to prevent the death of this beloved friend. But the important task from God's vantage point was to raise Lazarus from the dead. So Lazarus was allowed to die. Later Jesus revived him as a sign of his magnificent claim, "I am the resurrection and the life. He who believes in me will live, even though he dies" (John 11:25).

The truth is that we will be governed by pressures or by priorities. Either the pressures of the urgent or the priorities of the important will determine the outcome of our lives. The choice is ours.

LEARN TO SAY NO

Deciding what is important will keep you from falling into the trap of saying yes to everyone. The apostle Paul wrote, "To win the contest you must deny yourselves many things that would keep you from doing your best" (1 Cor. 9:25 LB). To make a difference in this world we must learn to say no to the lesser things in order to say yes to the greater things. This may be one of life's most difficult decisions.

Have you ever had someone ask you to serve on a committee or participate in a project, prefacing their request with, "It won't take much time"? So you say yes. Have you ever been given an opportunity that you just can't stand to miss out on? You rationalize and agree. "Somehow," you say, "I'll fit it in."

If we acquiesce all the time our schedules become more and more crowded. We soon lose touch with what is really important. We need help.

Living on the cutting edge mandates an ability to say no to many people and activities. Saying yes to true priorities will require that we say no to many other pursuits. E. Stanley Jones said, "Your capacity to say no determines your capacity to say yes to greater things." Or as one management consultant writes, "You have to decide what your highest priorities are and have the courage—pleasantly, smilingly, nonapologetically—to say 'no' to other things. And the way you do that is by having a bigger 'yes' burning inside."

Steven Covey, in his book *The Seven Habits of Highly Effective People,* tells an incident in his wife's life. She was invited to serve as chairperson of a committee in a community endeavor. She had a number of truly important things she was trying to work on, and she really didn't want to do it. But she felt pressured into it and finally agreed.

Then she called one of her dear friends to ask if she would serve on her committee. Her friend listened for a long time and then said, "Sandra, that sounds like a wonderful project, a really worthy undertaking. I appreciate so much your inviting me to be a part of it. I feel honored by it. For a number of reasons, I won't be participating myself, but I want you to know how much I appreciate your invitation."

Sandra was ready for anything but a pleasant "no." She turned to Steven and sighed, "I wish I'd said that."[5]

The ancient Chinese philosopher Mencius said, "Men must be decided on what they will not do, and then they are able to act with vigor in what they ought to do." You and I must decide what our highest priorities are. Then we can act on them without succumbing to the lesser pursuits of life.

MANAGE YOUR LIFE AND TIME

Deciding what is important will assist you in managing your life. A catchphrase today is time management. Actually that term is a misnomer. Time management is really life management. The challenge before us is not to manage our time, but to manage ourselves. Establishing our priorities will assist us in that endeavor.

A man got a call from his bank saying someone had deposited a thousand dollars in his name. In order to get it, all he had to do was come down, claim it, and spend it all that same day. The man, overjoyed, went down to pick up the money and had a fine time spending it.

But the next morning he got another call. Another thousand dollars. Same conditions. He sped down and repeated his efforts.

Third morning, same scenario. Now the man was getting a little concerned. He asked, "How long will this go on?"

The banker did not know. "This could be the last one today. It might not. I have no guarantees."

The man responded, "If this is going to keep happening, I'm going to have to do some planning. I can't just spend a thousand dollars every day of my life on a lark."

The banker agreed, but said that was his business.

The man sat down and tried to think of what to do. He didn't just want to dribble it all away, but he had to spend the full amount that day or it would be gone—lost forever—at the end.

What's the point? If you sleep about seven and half hours

a night, you have just about a thousand minutes to spend each day. You can't store them up or save them. You have to use them minute by minute.

What are we to do? The Scriptures say, "Be very careful, then, how you live—not as unwise but as wise, making the most of every opportunity, because the days are evil" (Eph. 5:15–16). To make the most of every opportunity or to redeem the time means to buy it back from another owner. We do this by scheduling our priorities, not by prioritizing what's on our schedule.

One of the most helpful things I was taught early in my career was to calendar my priorities. In other words, I get to my appointment calendar with my agenda before anybody else does. Sometimes this requires making personal commitments six to eight weeks in advance. Into my calendar I put the nonnegotiables of my life, my priorities: time alone with God, commitments to my family, sermon preparation, writing. Then I honor those appointments with as much importance as any other invitation. This practice has helped me immensely. When someone asks to meet with me at a time that would preclude my originally scheduled appointment to accomplish my priority I can easily say, "No, I already have a commitment at that time. Can we schedule it for another hour or another day?" But, and I repeat, the key is to schedule the priorities. In doing so, one is well on one's way to managing one's life.

FOCUS YOUR ENERGIES

Deciding what is important will enable you to focus your energies. The apostle Paul knew a great deal about priorities. He, other than Jesus, accomplished more for the cause of Christianity than any other person. But it wasn't without a great price. Here was an individual who established his priorities and then directed his efforts to accomplishing those goals. He summed up his life's purpose by saying, "One thing I do: Forgetting what is behind and straining toward what is ahead, I press on toward the goal to win the prize for which God has called me heavenward in Christ Jesus" (Phil. 3:13–14). Notice Paul did not say, "These forty things I dabble at." Rather, he stated, this "one thing I do." His life was based and revolved around his priority of growing in the likeness of Christ and reaching the world for Christ.

Jesus was the same way. People were always trying to sidetrack Jesus from his planned priorities. They tried to distract him from his purpose in life. On one occasion, "At daybreak Jesus went out to a solitary place. The people were looking for him and when they came to where he was, they tried to keep him from leaving them" (Luke 4:42). Jesus had planned to leave but they tried to get him to stay. Jesus responded, "I must preach the good news of the kingdom of God to the other towns also, because that is why I was sent" (Luke 4:43). He refused to be distracted. He knew his purpose and his agenda. He was persistent and focused in achieving that task.

When we diffuse our efforts, we are ineffective. When we concentrate our efforts, we are more effective. Diffused light falls harmlessly onto a piece of paper, but intensely focused, the same amount of light becomes a laser beam that can cut through steel. The same principle holds true for human effort. Diffused effort has little effect, but intense effort focused on a single goal can bring about startling results.

When I was in high school I played basketball, baseball, football, and tennis. I loved each sport. One day I overheard a coach say that the athletes that have a chance of making it to the next level, college athletics, must choose one sport to master. I assessed my skills and physical abilities in each sport and decided that if I had any chance of playing a sport in college, which was a dream of mine, that I must concentrate my efforts. I chose tennis. After a lot of hours of drills and work I became the number one player on the high school team. I received a scholarship to play collegiately, and two of the teams I played on went to the college national tournament. I recognized that while I was fairly gifted in athletics I knew that if I wanted to truly excel I had to focus on one sport. I did. And it paid off.

Likewise, in our spiritual and ministerial lives a focused and concentrated effort will produce maximum results.

PREVENT NEGATIVE INFLUENCE OF CONTROLLING PEOPLE

Deciding what is important will prevent the negative influence of controlling people. Umpire Marty Springstead's first major league appearance behind home plate was memorable. It was 1966 in Washington, D.C. that Frank Howard, the mountainous slugger of the Washington Senators, stepped up to the plate. The first pitch to Howard was a knee-high fast ball. Springstead called it a strike. Howard turned around and thundered at the rookie umpire, "Get something straight buster! I don't know where you came from or how you got to the major leagues, but they don't call that pitch on me a strike. Understand?" The next pitch was a knee-high fast ball. Springstead yelled, "Two!" "Two what?" roared Howard. "Too low, much too low," said Springstead.

Every now and then we meet people who want us to compromise our agendas, values, and priorities. These controlling people in our lives seem to think, "God loves you and I have a wonderful plan for your life."

At one church I served was a member who was one of the most fun-loving persons I had ever met. He was truly a joy to be around. He had a job that gave him enormous amounts of discretionary time. He often spent it by coming to visit me in my office, or coming by and taking me out to lunch, or on one of his local business trips, or any number of things he could come up with to pass his (and my) time away. While I thoroughly enjoyed his company, I soon discovered that important tasks that I needed to complete were being left unfinished. My weekly routine suffered miserably. I was digging a hole for myself. If I didn't do something I would be inundated with a multitude of unfinished projects and people calling for my attention.

My solution in this case was to express my priorities to this individual and to suggest that we schedule one day a week where we would meet for lunch. This arrangement would meet both of our agendas. We soon discovered that this was an excellent solution. This way we could still enjoy each other's companionship and I could finish my weekly tasks without feeling the pressure caused by a misuse of my time.

From this experience I discovered that people are important, and I am a person, therefore, I am important too. So to prevent dominating people from manipulating and controlling and dictating my schedule I had to determine what was priority. If these nonnegotiables were not firmly in place I was at the mercy of anyone who had a notion to visit, wanted my attendance at meetings, or wished for me to do something that was his or her responsibility to begin with.

In the people profession, I often think that I have to drop everything to be at everyone's beck and call. But that is not always true. The person who is always available is not always useful. If we are to help and encourage people we need time for our own replenishment and growth. To not schedule and guard those times hurts not only me but also the people I have been called to help.

Life places hundreds of opportunities before us for deciding what is important. Some choices are bad. Others are good. A few are the best. But each of us must decide, "What is my choice? What is my reason for living?" In other words, "What is priority in my life?"

What makes priorities so important? Chuck Swindoll wrote, "Life is a lot like a coin; you can spend it any way you wish, but you can spend it only once. Choosing one thing over all the rest throughout life is a difficult thing to do. This is especially true when the choices are so many and the possibilities are so close."[6] Yet in doing so we uncover a gold mine of possibilities and opportunities. Life will become more meaningful. We will be on our way to making a difference.

ENDNOTES

1. Mark R. Littleton, *Delighted By Discipline* (Wheaton: Victor Books, 1990), 126.

2. E. M. Gray, "The Common Denominator of Success," quoted in Stephen R. Covey, *The Seven Habits of Highly Effective People* (New York: Simon and Schuster, 1989), 148–149.

3. Richard C. Halverson, quoted in Edward R. Dayton and Ted W. Engstrom, *Strategy for Living* (Ventura: Regal Books, 1976), 180.

4. Ibid., 67.

5. Covey, *The Seven Habits of Highly Effective People*, 156.

6. Charles R. Swindoll, *Living Above the Level of Mediocrity* (Waco: Word Books, 1987), 109.

6

Prayer—*The Most Neglected Weapon in the War*

I needed a break. The demands of ministry were crashing in on me like a tidal wave. The responsibilities of leading a growing congregation were eating away at me like a rat chewing on a cord. My many commitments were crowding me into a prison of my own devising. I was depressed and worried. I decided to take time off to recuperate and unwind. But contrary to my expectations, each morning as I awoke, the demons of depression and worry were present. I could not shake them. My gloomy companions shadowed me everywhere I went until Wednesday morning. On that day I awoke and they had vanished. I relaxed and felt a deep peace. Not a single thing had changed, but everything was different.

On Friday I went to my mailbox. One piece of mail was a postcard from my home church. It read simply, "We prayed for you today. We asked that the burdens of your ministry would be lifted and you would experience the peace of God in a fresh and new way." It was dated two days before—Wednesday. The same day the demons of my prison had departed.

Those saintly and godly people of my home church had

gathered in a simple and probably unexciting prayer meeting. Yet they had unleashed the most powerful weapon in a believer's arsenal. The weapon of prayer is an unstoppable source of power.

I graduated from high school as the Vietnam War was coming to a painful close. When our nation entered the war that was fought in the desert of Iraq and Kuwait I was overwhelmed at the weapons of this warfare. The Tomahawk cruise missiles, SCUD missiles, Challenger tanks, Cobra attack helicopters, Abrams M-1A1 tanks, Stealth bombers, F-15s, AWACS, Toronados, B-52s, to name only a few, made a profound impression on me. Each evening as the videos were viewed on the nightly news I was amazed at the power and sophistication of our military's weaponry. The awesomeness of these weapons brought the Iraqi government to its knees.

Christian leaders are fighting a war too. A spiritual war. And we too have weapons at our disposal. "For the weapons of our warfare are not of the flesh, but divinely powerful for the destruction of fortresses" (2 Cor. 10:4 NASB). What are the weapons in the Christian's arsenal? Paul instructs us in Ephesians 6 to put on the full armor of God. Our battle is not against flesh and blood but against the spiritual forces of evil.

He then lists both defensive and offensive weapons. It is one of the offensive weapons I want to dismantle and put together again. "Take . . . the sword of the Spirit, which is the *word of God*. And *pray* in the Spirit on all occasions with all kinds of prayers and requests" (Eph. 6:17–18). Paul informs us that when we Christians engage in battle we have two weapons at our disposal—God's Word and prayer.

In a sense these offensive and constructive weapons are two lanes on the same road. When we read God's Word he talks to us. When we pray we speak to God. In doing so, we turn the key that unlocks God's prevailing power in our lives that brings the demonic enemies to their knees.

How do we discharge this powerful weapon? The weaponry of our armed forces is highly technical and complex. But not prayer. I think we would like to make it complex. But it is not. Actually, it is amazingly simple, as my home church demonstrated. In fact, we do not need more information as much as we need inspiration to hurl this powerful and potent missile at the Enemy.

For analyzing the purposes of this powerful weapon, let's examine the life of an Old Testament character who is relatively obscure. His life story takes up only two verses. If you read fast you might pass over him unnoticed. His name is Jabez, which sounds like the Hebrew for "pain." His account is found in 1 Chronicles 4:9–10.

Jabez was more honorable than his brothers. His mother had named him Jabez, saying, "'I gave birth to him in pain.' Jabez cried out to the God of Israel, 'Oh that you would bless me and enlarge my territory! Let your hand be with me, and keep me from harm so that I will be free from pain.' And God granted his request" (1 Chron. 4:9–10).

From his example we discover how to unleash the powerful weapon of prayer.

PRAY PRIVATELY

I get the sneaking suspicion that Jabez would often slip off alone to pray. Solitude was, and is, the beginning place of powerful prayer. Obviously, one can pray anywhere anytime. Praying privately does not rule out public prayer. The point is that sustained, continued response in our prayer lives necessitates a time of private devotion.

Some people pray in public places, at social gatherings, and at mealtimes just so they can be seen and heard and assumed to be religious. But prayer is not a spectator sport. It was never intended for public display. Nor was it intended for religious theatrics.

Why the emphasis on privacy? The practical reason is because a private place insures a minimum of distractions. Distractions can be deadly when it comes to making contact with the Father. But the main reason for privacy is because prayer is meeting with God face-to-face and friend-to-friend.

For me, my private place is the sofa in my office. I arrive early before the phones start ringing or uninvited interruptions begin. I enter my private sanctuary to speak and listen to God. My private place becomes a holy place. I meet God there.

PRAY CONSISTENTLY

Among the myriad of names, over five hundred in all, tucked away in the first few chapters of 1 Chronicles, the name of Jabez stands out. This man gained the attention of the chronicler. Why? Because this man had a reputation. One is known for what he or she does the most. And Jabez was known as a man of prayer. "Jabez cried out to the God of Israel" (v. 10). He had made prayer not only a habit, but a way of life.

The apostle Paul made a profound and positive impact upon the world for the kingdom of God. How? He was in contact with God and God was in touch with him. He modeled what he wrote, "Pray without ceasing" (1 Thess. 5:17 NASB). He made prayer a way of life.

John Hyde of India made prayer such a dominant characteristic of his life that he was nicknamed "Praying Hyde." Because he employed the weapon of prayer, Christianity made substantial inroads into the country of India. John Hyde made prayer a way of life.

George Müller, a native of Germany, did not believe there was a God until he was twenty-one. When he was converted he instantly decided to give his life to his new-found Christ. A few years later he moved to Bristol, England. He began the work for which he was to become famous—the care of orphans. He began with a handful of children and soon there were as many as 2,100 children.

Through the years this man actually prayed for every need every day. He kept a diary. He told no one of his needs. He did not have someone in charge of raising money. He did not publish a brochure. He did not have any direct mail campaigns. He simply told the Lord: "I need this for your work."

The Lord provided him 7.5 million dollars. He educated 123,000 students throughout the world. He supported 189 missionaries. He hired 112 men and women as assistants.

George Müller was an ordinary man with an extraordinary prayer life. He made prayer a way of life.

What was the distinctive of these men's lives? Prayer. What was the result of these men's lives? Power. These people had power in their lives because they made prayer a way of life. God's power flows primarily to people who pray. It has been said, "When we work, we work; but when we pray, God works." An English archbishop once observed, "It's amazing how many coincidences occur when one begins to pray."

PRAY SPECIFICALLY

Next, let's examine the content of Jabez's prayer. Some commentators indicate that this is a selfish prayer. Others say it is an unchristian prayer. Granted, there is more to prayer than what Jabez prayed. But it does provide us with an example of specific prayer. There are four parts to his prayer.

First, Jabez prayed, "Oh that you would bless me." How often have you heard someone pray using the word *bless*? People often pray asking God to bless their lives, the food, the offering, and the church. What does it mean to ask for God's blessing? In a biblical sense, a blessing is an act of God by which he causes someone or something to supernaturally produce more than would be naturally possible. You see, the normal Christian life is a supernatural life. The ordinary is the extraordinary.

Second, Jabez prayed, "And enlarge my territory." A man's territory marks the limit of his influence. This was a prayer for lengthened influence and heightened opportunity. One of the certain signs of ministry on the cutting edge is the desire for greater influence. Dawson Trotman, the founder of the Navigators, stated, "It brings no honor to God to ask for peanuts, when he wants to give us continents." Phillips Brooks wrote, "Pray the largest prayers. You cannot think a prayer so large that God, in answering it, will not wish you had made it larger. Pray not for crutches but for wings." The prayer of influence can be accomplished by following a strategy I have found useful: Pray Big, Start Small, Get Going. Praying big honors God. Starting small recognizes our humanness. Getting going affirms our faith.

Third, Jabez prayed, "Let your hand be with me." God's hand is a picture of God's guidance in one's life. How foolish to ask for God's blessing and lengthened influence without God's hand of leadership and direction. Jabez was not on a power trip. He was giving God a free hand with his life. He was asking to be controlled, directed, and taken over by the hand of God.

Fourth, Jabez prayed, "And keep me from harm so that I will be free from pain." Jabez is not praying that evil might be kept from him, but that he might be kept from evil. He is not praying that he would not be exposed to evil but that he would not succumb to evil. Just as Jesus instructed in the model prayer, "Lead us not into temptation, but deliver us from the evil one" (Matt. 6:13), Jabez was requesting God's protection.

The characteristic of Jabez's life is that he prayed. The characteristic of his prayer is that it was specific. A powerful prayer is a specific prayer. A weapon is useless if it does not know its target or is not aimed toward its target. Intercessory prayer fails to hit the mark if it is not a specific request. Answers to vague and general prayers are few.

In one church I served, Ted, an attorney, was asked to pray for the offering. He spoke, "Lord, use this money to reach more people for Christ. Amen." At first, I thought it was a joke. A few weeks later, he was called on to pray the invocation. He prayed, "Lord, speak to each person through this service. Amen." Simple and specific.

Praying specifically places our words right before God. To insure specific prayers I began a few years ago writing out my prayers each day during my devotional time. At first this was difficult, but as time went on I became more focused and directed in my prayers. No longer was I requesting vague generalities but rather in meaningful specifics. After several months of prayer writing, I reviewed my entries. God had been up to something. I began to see how he was answering many of my prayers. Not that they all were answered in my timing or in the way I had wanted, but my prayers were answered.

PRAY EXPECTANTLY

Jabez prayed. God answered. "And God granted his request." Answered prayer is not abnormal; it is normal. It is not unusual; it can be an everyday experience. It is not to be marveled at, but to be expected.

I think one of the major reasons God does not answer my prayers is because I do not expect him to. Perhaps the most difficult element of prayer is not asking but believing. Early in my Christian walk I asked a trusted and faithful man of God why none of my prayers were being answered. I had been praying consistently for my friends to come to Christ.

With years of experience and wisdom, the man replied, "Well, young whippersnapper, who do you think you are? You don't expect everything you pray for to be answered just because you pray for it, do you?"

"Well, no sir," I stammered, "I guess not."

"Then that," replied the man, "is the very reason they're not."

Faith is essential to effective, powerful prayer. Faith is not believing God can. Faith is believing God will. And, like a muscle, faith grows stronger with use.

The Bible says, "And everything you ask in prayer, believing, you shall receive" (Matt. 21:22 NASB). "All things are possible to him who believes" (Mark 9:23 NASB). "I say to you, all things for which you pray and ask, believe that you have received them, and they shall be granted you" (Mark 11:24 NASB).

You may be saying that you just don't have enough faith. But the truth is that we don't need more faith. We need to appropriate the faith we already have. Our problem lies not in the amount of faith, but the direction it is pointed. Jesus said, "Whoever says to this mountain, 'Be taken up and cast into the sea,' and does not doubt in his heart, but believes that what he says is going to happen, it shall be granted him" (Mark 11:23 NASB). Faith comes not by looking at the Enemy, but by looking at God.

Granted, we must understand that those answers may not come in the way we request or in the timing that is congruent with our wills. But our specific prayers will be answered. We must always remember that a no and a not yet are just as clear an answer as a go for it. God still reigns supreme. He is still on his throne. He sees the whole picture of our lives. We must understand that he knows best and answers our prayers correctly. So when we are right spiritually before God, God's plan will be fullfilled. God's timing is correct, and when our faith is focused on God, we can see results and answers to our prayers.

One of my first speaking experiences came in a big way.

As a junior in high school, I was invited to speak before four thousand people at a Lane Adams crusade being held in a local football stadium. Lane Adams at the time was an associate evangelist of Billy Graham. I had returned recently from a youth convention in Dallas, Texas called Explo '72. A college freshman and I were asked to share our experiences at the convention attended by over a hundred thousand high school and college students. Needless to say I was scared to death. Thousands of people and Lane Adams would hear me. "I'm going to make a fool of myself," I thought. This would be a disaster. The mountain of people loomed large. Satan was telling me that I was going to look like a fool. I prayed but all I could muster were doubt-filled prayers.

The college student must have noticed my knees shaking and my palms sweating. She leaned over before I spoke and said, "Remember God is great. God is faithful. Don't look at the size of the crowd; remember our great God." At that moment I changed my focus. I stopped looking at myself and at the mountain of people. I closed my mind to the sultry voice of the Evil One. I began to focus on the mountain mover. I began to trust in God to use me.

The missile of prayer found its target. The Devil was silenced. The crowd still looked just as big, but I knew that God was bigger. Many people came to Christ that evening. And this high-school boy learned to believe in a powerful God that can answer prayer.

7

Worship—The Missing Jewel of the Leader's Life

A small boy sat beside his mother in church. Like most children, his attention was neither easily captured nor readily held. So much of what was happening in the service seemed uninteresting, unrelated, unimportant. Quite frankly, he was bored stiff! Suddenly his ever-wandering eyes noticed a bronze plaque prominently placed upon the side wall. There he saw stars, letters, and the outline of an American flag. Nudging his mother and pointing to the plaque, he asked, "What's that?" Graciously and patiently the young mother replied, "Oh, those are the names of people from our church who died in the service."

There was a long pause. Suddenly he demanded his mother's attention again. With a sense of concern—almost panic—he asked, "Mom, was that in the first or the second service?"

Is it safe to say that true, life-changing, energetic worship that acknowledges the power and presence of the living God is missing from many evangelical churches and their leaders. Suffice it to say that we can't be effective as leaders without continual doses of the worship of an all-sufficient and all-loving God. Worship is to the Christian's life what the mainspring is to a watch, what the engine is to a car. It is the very core, the most essential element.

The greatest need among Christian leaders today is not new programs. It is not a new analysis of population distribution. It is not an innovative electronic gadget. It is not an enlightening conference or seminar. It is not new mechanics. What we desperately need is to gain a life-changing glimpse of the greatness, the awesomeness, the wonder, the power, the mercy, the goodness, and the loving-kindness of the God we serve. And that glimpse is caught through worship. To miss worship is to miss life itself. A. W. Tozer wrote, "Worship is the missing jewel of the evangelical church. . . . The greatest tragedy in the world today is that God has made man in His image and made him to worship Him, made him to play the harp of worship before the face of God day and night, but he has failed God and dropped the harp. It lies voiceless at his feet."[1] Robert Webber wrote a book a few years ago titled, *Worship Is A Verb*. If worship is active, what exactly does worship do?

WORSHIP BRINGS OUR HEARTS TO GOD

The most often used word for worship in the Greek New Testament is *proskeno*. Jesus used this word when he confronted one of Satan's temptations. "Worship the Lord your God, and serve him only" (Matt. 4:10). Jesus also uttered this word in his conversation with the woman at the well, "God is spirit, and his worshipers must worship in spirit and in truth" (John 4:24). This word means "to kiss toward," or "to kiss the hand," or "to bow down." It embodies the idea of blowing a kiss. It is a term of affection and adoration. We come close to its meaning when we say, "I worship the ground she walks on."

A teacher once explained the adoration aspect of worship to a college class. A student asked what worship was really like. He couldn't understand why God would command such a thing nor how an individual could continually give it.

"Think back," the teacher told him, "to the time when you first fell in love. Do you remember what it felt like?"

The student's smile told him that he did.

"Do you remember how beautiful she was?"

He nodded.

"Did you ever tell her so?"

"Of course!" he said. "I couldn't stop telling her."

"Did you enjoy telling her?"

"It was a pleasure."

"Now take that pleasure, and the beauty that inspired it, and multiply it by infinity," he said. "Take those words of loving admiration, and multiply them by eternity. That's how beautiful God is, how delightful it is to praise him, and how long you will want to do it. That's worship."

The class burst into applause, the student's eyes filled with tears, and a lump rose in the teacher's throat. This student was on his way to knowing firsthand what it meant to bring one's heart to God.

Worship is not a weekly pep talk to rally the troops and win the contest. Worship is not the Christian alternative to a Saturday night rock concert. Worship takes place when people who have fallen in love with the God of the universe come together and express that love through singing, prayers, Bible readings, offerings, and proclamation.

WORSHIP CALLS US BACK TO THE CENTER

A young stranger to the Alps was making his first climb, accompanied by two stalwart guides. It was a steep, hazardous ascent, but he felt secure with one guide ahead and one following. For hours they climbed. And now, breathless, they reached for those rocks protruding through the snow above them—the summit.

The guide ahead wished to let the stranger have the first glorious view of heaven and earth, and moved aside to let him go first. Forgetting the gales that would blow across those summit rocks, the young man leaped to his feet. But the chief guide dragged him down. "On your knees, sir!" he shouted. "You are never safe here except on your knees."[2]

Worship calls us back to the center where life is focused and in harmony. On our knees there is a place of safety where all is in order, a place from which comes the energy that overcomes turbulence and is not intimidated by it. In Biblical language this place is referred to as the heart. The writer of Proverbs wrote, "Above all else, guard your heart, for it is the wellspring of life" (Prov. 4:23). Paul wrote, "And the peace of God, which transcends all understanding, will guard your hearts and your minds in Christ Jesus" (Phil. 4:7). The heart is the inmost center of an individual, the seat of one's will, intellect, and emotions. It is the center from which all human activity proceeds. In both verses, we are commanded to guard our hearts. In other words, we are to garrison or establish a sentry at the doorway of the heart, the center of our existence.

How can we guard our hearts? Only one way—through the worship of God. Worship calls us back to the center. It reminds us who is in control and who is the force of life. Without worship we become focused on the periphery of life and ministry—budget, baptisms, and buildings. The things in our external world become more important than what takes place at the seat of our wills and emotions. Not to worship is to become frazzled and distraught. To worship is to live in peace and contentment.

Paul reminds us again to "Set your minds on things above, not on earthly things. . . . Let the peace of Christ rule in your hearts" (Col. 3:2, 15). When we worship and put Christ at the center of our lives there will be peace. The worshipful Christian will always be governed by peace. We won't worry when we are worshiping.

WORSHIP CHANGES US INTO THE LIKENESS OF CHRIST

In a real sense we become what we worship. If we go after worthlessness, we will become worthless. If we give ourselves to things that do not profit, we become unprofitable. If we worship less than God himself, we will become less than God intended us to be. Human beings tend to become like the object of their mental and emotional focus. We slowly change to become like the center of our psychological world.

Have you ever noticed that when a daughter resents her mother over a long period of time, that resentment keeps the child's thoughts and feelings locked onto the parent? She may say, "I'll never be like my mom," yet, ironically, the daughter usually ends up with the same character flaws that made the mother a source of resentment in the first place. The girl is changed into the image of the center of her psychological world.

Or what about the little boy who idolizes violent film characters? In time, he tends to become aggressive, perhaps even violent, like the character he admires.

Yet, on the positive side, worshiping the Lord rivets our heart's gaze on him. The result is a likeness to God himself. The apostle Paul stated it this way, "And we, who with unveiled faces all reflect the Lord's glory, are being transformed into his likeness with ever-increasing glory" (2 Cor. 3:18). When we worship God, something marvelous happens: we begin to reflect what God is like.

Many years ago some men were panning for gold in Montana, and one of them found an unusual stone. Breaking it open, he was excited to see that it contained gold. Working eagerly, the men soon discovered an abundance of the precious metal. Happily, they began shouting with delight, "We've found it! We've found gold! We're rich!" They had to interrupt their celebrating though, to go into a nearby town and stock up on supplies. Before they left camp, the men agreed not to tell a soul about their find. Indeed, no one breathed a word about it to anyone while they were in town. Much to their dismay, however, when they were about to return, hundreds of men were prepared to follow them. When they asked the crowd to tell who "squealed," the reply came, "No one had to. Your faces showed it!"

Our lives are like mirrors. We reflect what we worship. And when we worship God, we reflect his glory and his nature. It is written all over our faces.

WORSHIP CLARIFIES OUR PERSPECTIVE

One of the greatest benefits of worship is that it clarifies our vision. It allows us to see our lives and ministries from a new perspective. Worship not only puts us in touch with the presence of God, it also puts us in the place with God. When we exalt God, we gain two life-changing perspectives.

We gain a view of the throne of God. When we come into the presence of God we see him as Isaiah did, "seated on a throne, high and exalted, and the train of his robe filled the temple" (Isa. 6:1). To see God reigning in power, wisdom, and love produces only one response from us—awe.

It is like watching a breathtaking landscape—perhaps a shimmering range of snow-covered mountains or a glorious sunset over the ocean. We cannot remain silent. We exclaim, "Wow! How beautiful!" To remain silent in the presence of such beauty seems wrong. Likewise, not to express admiration and love in the presence of God is wrong. When we view the throne of God, it is only right and fitting to worship him.

Another perspective we gain from worship might be called a view from the throne of God. When we worship, we realize that we are, as the apostle Paul says, "seated . . . with him in the heavenly realms in Christ Jesus" (Eph. 2:6). Through worship we take a position above the world, ourselves, our circumstances, and our problems.

When we behold God in worship, we look on our world from his perspective. We find what we thought was a mountain is only a molehill. What seems great and mighty in the world's eyes turns out to be small and insignificant in God's eyes. On the other hand, what we thought was weak, we learn is actually strong; what we thought foolish is wise.

WORSHIP IS AN ALL-THE-TIME THING

Worship is not something we do an hour each Sunday or a few minutes each day in a devotional time. Worship is a way of life. It is something we do all the time.

The completeness of worship is expressed in the words of an elderly gentleman who once prayed at a midweek church meeting:

> O Lord, we will praise you; we will praise you
> with an instrument of ten strings.
> We will praise you with our two eyes
> by looking only to you.
> We will exalt you with our two ears
> by listening only to your voice.
> We will extol you with our two hands
> by working in your service.
> We will honor you with our two feet
> by walking in the way of your statutes.
> We will magnify you with our tongues
> by bearing testimony to your lovingkindness.
> We will worship you with our hearts
> by loving you.

We thank you for this instrument, Lord.
Keep it in tune.
Play upon it as you will and ring out
the melodies of your grace.
May its harmonies always express your glory.

This "instrument of ten strings" is summarized in Scripture: "Therefore, I urge you, brothers, in view of God's mercy, to offer your bodies as living sacrifices, holy and pleasing to God—which is your spiritual worship" (Rom. 12:1). Worship is not just singing a few songs and listening to a message; worship entails the giving of our bodies, our time, our possessions, as well as the giving of our minds, our emotions, and our wills in holy obedience to God.

John MacArthur, in *The Ultimate Priority*, wrote, "That consuming, selfless desire to give to God is the essence and the heart of worship. It begins with the giving first of ourselves, and then of our attitudes, and then of our possessions—until worship is a way of life."[3] The fact remains, unless we are prepared to worship God with all of our lives, we will find it nearly impossible to worship God for one hour on Sunday.

In the grand scheme of things worship should change us. If we are not changed after we have worshiped, it has not been worship. To worship is to change—to change actions, to change attitudes, to change minds, to change directions, to change perspectives, to change character, to change devotion, to change ourselves. If worship does not propel us into greater obedience, we have not worshiped.

It has been said that too many Christians worship their work, work at their play, and play at their worship. When I understand that worship isn't just a service I attend but a life I live before God, then I am well on my way toward fulfilling God's plan for my life.

ENDNOTES

1. A. W. Tozer, *Worship: The Missing Jewel* (Camp Hill, Pa.: Christian Publications, 1992), 8.

2. Craig Brian Larson, ed., *Illustrations for Preaching and Teaching* (Grand Rapids: Baker Books, 1993), 281.

3. John MacArthur, *The Ultimate Priority* (Chicago: Moody Press, 1983), 14.

8

Leadership—
The Common Denominator

"I'm no orator," Theodore Roosevelt once said, "and in writing I'm afraid I'm not gifted at all. . . . If I have anything at all resembling genius it is the gift for leadership." That gift propelled him to the presidency at age forty-two, making him the youngest man ever to occupy that office, to the anger and astonishment of a good many older politicians who thought themselves far better equipped than he for power. It is easy to see how they were led to underestimate him.

There was nothing physically attractive about Theodore Roosevelt. He stood no taller than five feet, nine inches, and was built like a barrel. His blue eyes squinted out nearsightedly through pince-nez, and his brown moustache framed teeth so large and white they sometimes frightened friends as well as enemies. His voice was high-pitched, even squeaky.

Yet, the vivid force of his character and personality, his unabashed, contagious joy in taking charge made the difference. He was a leader of monumental proportions. A political foe called him "a steam-engine in trousers." A British visitor thought him comparable only to Niagara Falls among the natural wonders of the New World. His ability to lead—and the rugged, restless, constitution that went along with it—was not really a gift at all, but a hard-won achievement. To an extraordinary degree, Theodore Roosevelt was his own creation.

He was just fifty when he left the White House, and only sixty-one when he died on January 5, 1919. As the pallbearers carried his coffin through the snow-covered trees to a hilltop grave at Oyster Bay, and the family followed along behind it, a New York police captain said to his sister: "Do you remember the fun of him, Mrs. Robinson? It was not only that he was a great man, but, oh, there was such fun in being led by him."[1]

I would like to be a leader like that: one whom my constituents would have fun in following. As I have studied leadership—the common denominator of organizations, churches, and families living on the cutting edge—I have discovered that being an effective leader is neither easy nor accidental. Effective leaders are made not born. They are those rare individuals who know where they are going, communicate that purpose to others, and fuel the fires that bring others alongside of them. They are truly a joy to follow.

Theodore Roosevelt was that kind of leader. So too was the cupbearer for King Artaxerxes in Susa, a man by the name of Nehemiah. After receiving word that the Jews in Jerusalem were distressed because they were defenseless without a wall, he made plans to return there to lead the people in rebuilding the wall. He accomplished a remarkable feat with a formerly depressed and defeated people. In a few short weeks the wall was completed amid conditions that were far from good—attacks from opponents, and problems left and right. Yet, this man, like Teddy Roosevelt, welded an unstoppable force.

God has always been in the business of working through men and women to accomplish seemingly impossible tasks. God looks to those individuals who are not afraid to believe in him in spite of overwhelming odds. Nehemiah proved to be that kind of man. From his story we discover the marks of an effective leader—the kind of person God can use.

PLANNING

God uses the person who plans. God has always used those people with dreams and visions for doing a great work for his glory. Leadership begins with visionary plans. Absolutely nothing happens until someone starts dreaming.

Such a dreamer was Nehemiah. "I hadn't told a soul about *the plans* for Jerusalem which God had put into my heart" (Neh. 2:12 LB). God was putting a great vision in the mind of Nehemiah. Nehemiah's plans were of divine design. He had spent time with God, consulting with the master architect, formulating a plan that was pleasing to God and acceptable to the people.

God put into his heart what he was to do. It has been said, "Only those who can see the invisible can attempt the impossible." Nehemiah saw the wall built before it was built. In other words, Nehemiah created the wall twice—once mentally, then physically. In his mind's eye he was able to draw the design, the plan, that God intended for the city.

Do we plan with the same intensity as Nehemiah? Do we go before God asking him to reveal his plans for our ministries, our lives, our families? As leaders, if we don't plan, then who will? It has been said that those who fail to plan, plan to fail. No one intentionally sets out to fail. Yet when you and I put our plans down on paper we are more apt to succeed. Plans are essential for accomplishing our goals. Even the Scriptures emphasize this need in leading. The writer of Proverbs says, "We should make plans—counting on God to direct us" (Prov. 16:9 LB), and, "The wise man looks ahead" (Prov. 14:8 LB).

Planning is mandatory for progress. A friend used to tell me, "Proper planning prevents poor performance." I am continually amazed at the number of churches and Christian organizations that operate under the "*que sera sera*"—what ever will be will be—attitude. Such organizations have taken a defensive strategy that will leave them eating the dust of others who take the offensive and plan.

Furthermore, when we fail to plan we spend our time reacting rather than acting. We are going to be controlled by either pressures or plans. When we choose to plan we take charge and control of our lives. All too often when leaders fail to plan properly, they are forced to do what I call "panic planning." The pressures of the moment demand action and we are ill-equipped. Contrary to popular opinion, no one works well under pressure.

Nehemiah was controlled by plans. And if you look closely you will notice that his plan had three parts. An effective plan always has these three ingredients.

1. *The What.* This is the goal. Nehemiah's goal was, plain and simple, to build the wall around Jerusalem. He knew this part even before he came to Jerusalem. What are your goals? What do you want to accomplish in your area of leadership? By the way, this is the easy step for making plans, but this step alone is incomplete without steps two and three.

2. *The How.* This is the hard part. We may say, I want to raise godly kids or make a million dollars or build a great Bible study class. Yet we attempt our dream and fall flat on our faces. We then say that God must not have fostered this dream when the truth is we have not invested the time to develop the how of the plan. The how is the strategy.

Notice what Nehemiah did when he first arrived in Jerusalem. Did he immediately start building the wall? No. He spent three days inspecting the ruins. The word *inspecting* means to look at something very carefully. It's a medical word for probing a wound to see the extent of the damage. Nehemiah knew the what of the plan but not the how until he surveyed the damage. A leader who makes effective plans always does his homework. This is what Nehemiah was doing by inspecting the wall.

Often we hear the misguided counsel, "Don't just sit there, do something." But frequently this is incorrect. When we don't know what to do first, the counsel is best stated, "Don't just do something, sit there." This is what Nehemiah did, and what we should do too if we want to be effective.

3. *The When.* Nehemiah knew what he was to do. He now had the facts on how to accomplish the task. But the plan was still not complete without the when. This is the timing of the plan. We may have the greatest God-honoring dream, the most methodical and detailed plan, but without God's timing it will be nothing more than human ingenuity and creativity attempting to accomplish God's plan. If you want God's plan to succeed, then you must always wait on his timing. The leader sets the tone of the organization by his plans.

INSPIRING

God uses the person who motivates others. It has been said, "There are three kinds of people in the world—those who don't know what's happening, those who watch what's happening, and those who make things happen." A leader is one who has a fire burning in his heart and can set other people on fire without making them burn. In other words, an effective leader motives people to action.

A leader has been defined as someone who knows the road, who can keep ahead, and who can pull others after him. The people who make an impact on the world are not necessarily the geniuses, or the best looking, or the most talented, but those who can inspire others to action. In its simplest terms, leadership is influence. People don't follow programs, they follow leaders who inspire them.

Nehemiah had that remarkable ability to influence and inspire and rally people to action. "But now I told them, 'You know full well the tragedy of our city; it lies in ruins and its gates are burned. Let us rebuild the wall of Jerusalem and rid ourselves of this disgrace!'

"Then I told them about the desire God had put into my heart, and of my conversation with the king, and the plan to which he had agreed.

"They replied at once, 'Good! Let's rebuild the wall!' And so the work began" (Neh. 2:17–18 LB).

Remember these are the same defeated people in the same difficult situation. The only difference was one man with God's vision who motivated others to put their hearts into the work. Nehemiah possessed the quality that could bring out the best in others.

Have you ever wondered at the way certain people bring out the best in others? We have all known them—coaches, teachers, parents, bosses. They seem to possess a knack for inspiring people. And this remarkable skill in the art of motivation makes them successful at almost everything they do.

All of us at one time or another are called upon to inspire others. The following are some key principles of motivation that can be mastered by anyone with the desire to inspire others.

1. *Identify with the people.* Notice that Nehemiah didn't say look at the terrible situation "you" are in, but look at the

terrible situation "we" are in. If you want to get someone to look at a problem from your point of view, you don't stand across from him and yell, you go to his side and identify with him and then gently guide him to your side.

2. *Acknowledge the seriousness of the situation.* Nehemiah didn't hide anything from the people or try to sugarcoat the problem. He honestly faced the facts.

3. *Appeal for action.* Nehemiah challenged the people to specific action: "Let us rebuild the wall." He had pondered and discussed and investigated and planned and prayed long enough. It was time for action. Let's begin the work.

4. *Assign the tasks.* Now the people were ready to hear the plan God had placed in his heart. Chapter 3 detailed the assignments for each family in rebuilding the wall. Nehemiah knew that a few people working alone could not rebuild it. But together, united in force, the task could be accomplished. The effective leader has the ability to cut the problems down to size. This is what Nehemiah did. He assigned each family a task that they could manage.

Nehemiah was a motivator. There is one sure test to see if we are motivators and that is, Is anyone following? Too often we are like the youth leader who said, "There goes my group. I must catch up with them. I am their leader."

The history books are filled with men and women who made a difference in their world by motivating others to action. Wellington reportedly said that when Napoleon was on the field, it was, in balance, the equivalent of fighting against another forty thousand men. During World War II the world watched, expecting Hitler to topple England in a few short weeks. But one man made a difference. Winston Churchill. At sixty-five he became prime minister after an erratic and frustrating career filled with failures. Churchill rallied the nation with his stirring speeches. You can almost hear his words again: "We shall go on to the end, we shall fight in France, we shall fight on the seas and oceans, we shall fight with growing confidence and growing strength in the air, we shall defend our island, whatever the cost may be, we shall fight on the beaches, we shall fight on the landing grounds, we shall fight in the fields and in the streets, we shall fight in the hills; we shall never surrender." And two weeks later, he proclaimed: "Let us therefore brace ourselves to our duties and so bear ourselves that if the British Empire and its Commonwealth last for a thousand years men will still say, 'This was their finest hour.'"[2]

The Green Bay Packers had been hapless for twelve years before their new coach, Vince Lombardi, arrived on the scene in 1959. Lombardi turned this team into the dominant NFL team of the 1960s.

How does one account for such a phenomenal turnaround? Frank Gifford says it was not Lombardi's knowledge, since several coaches knew as much about strategy and tactics. Rather, it was his ability to motivate the players. "He could get that extra ten percent out of an individual," Gifford says. "Multiply ten percent times forty men on the team times fourteen games a season—and you're going to win."

THICK SKIN

God uses the person who withstands criticism. Leadership has a price tag; and that price tag is criticism. A leader must learn to handle criticism. Whenever we are out front, people are going to take shots at us. No leader is exempt from it. In fact, the only way to avoid criticism is by saying nothing, doing nothing, and being nothing. Mark my words, the person ministering on the cutting edge will be criticized. Therefore, a leader must have thick skin. Stuart Briscoe writes, "Qualifications of a pastor (or any Christian leader): the mind of a scholar, the heart of a child, and the hide of a rhinoceros."[3]

Nehemiah needed thick skin and he had it. "But when Sanballat and Tobiah and Geshem the Arab heard of our plan, they scoffed" (Neh. 2:19 LB). Scoffing or mocking means "to utter repeatedly words of criticism." And these critics uttered their criticisms throughout the entire building project and even after it was completed.

Have you ever had people like that in your life? I have. It reminds me of a story. I do not know if it is true or not. But supposedly when Robert Fulton was building his steam engine, his wife came to him in his workshop and said, "You'll never get that thing to work and even if you do you'll never be able to get it out." Well, miraculously, according to his wife, he got it to work. The engine sat in his front yard as he worked to fit it on a boat. His wife came to him and said, "I don't know why you are spending so much time on that thing, you'll never get it to the river." Well, miraculously, according to his wife, he got the steam engine attached to a boat and got it down to the river. His wife came down to the river and said, "I don't know why you are wasting your time, you'll never get that thing to start." Well, miraculously, it did start and Fulton began moving down the river. He was happy on two accounts: one, his invention worked, and, two, he left his wife back on the dock. But just then, he heard a voice calling out from the bank. It was his wife running after him saying, "You'll never get that thing stopped. You never will."

Nehemiah knew what Robert Fulton felt. His critics never left him alone. They continued to hound and scoff and ridicule him day in and day out. They were a constant thorn in his side.

Leaders will be criticized. It comes with the territory. So how does one react when criticism comes?

1. *Talk to God about it.* I remember a song from my youth. The words of the chorus were, "You can talk about me whenever you please, but I'll talk about you when I am on my knees." Our first response to criticism is to take it to the Lord in prayer. Never tackle the criticism alone. Give it all away to God. He is the Chief Shepherd. Allow him to take the brunt of the attack.

2. *Learn from it.* Sometimes there is an element of truth in the criticism. We must shake out the kernels of truth and use them to help us grow.

3. *Use it to motivate you to greater action.* Often when I am criticized I employ it to spur me on to greater accomplishment. I know it is my competitive nature that sparks this reaction. But I have learned that I must take the criticism through the previously mentioned steps before I employ this response.

4. *Ignore it.* Sometimes one must consider the source. If the critic is someone who is critical of everyone and everything, then dismiss it and move on. Henry Ironside lived by this advice: "If what they are saying about you is true, mend your ways. It isn't true, forget it, and go on and serve the Lord."

Remember, people don't build statues to the critics, only to those who withstand the criticism to accomplish their God-given dreams. The first American steamboat took thirty-two hours to go from New York to Albany. People mocked. The horse and buggy passed the early motorcar as if it were standing still. (It usually was.) People mocked. The first electric light bulb was so dim people had to use a gas lamp to see it. They mocked. The first airplane came down fifty-nine seconds after it left the ground. People mocked. But where would we be today without those inventions. The critic is soon forgotten. The person of action is remembered.

In fulfilling God-given dreams and goals, people will discourage you and criticize you and ridicule you. That's a fact. But to hear from Theodore Roosevelt again:

> It is not the critic who counts; not the man who points out how the strong man stumbles, or where the doer of deeds could have done them better. The credit belongs to the man who is actually in the arena, whose face is marred by dust and sweat and blood; who strives valiantly; who errs, and comes short again and again, because there is no effort without error and shortcoming; but who does actually strive to do the deeds; who knows the great enthusiasms, the great devotions; who spends himself in a worthy cause; who at the best knows in the end the triumph of high achievement, and who at the worst, if he fails, at least fails while daring greatly.[4]

> Far better it is to dare mighty things, to win glorious triumphs, even though checkered by failure, than to take rank with those poor spirits who neither enjoy much nor suffer much, because they live in the gray twilight that knows not victory nor defeat.[5]

Let's go for the victory and leave the critics eating our dust.

THE FAITH FACTOR

God uses the person of faith. The Bible says, "Without faith it is impossible to please Him" (Heb. 11:6 NASB).

Nehemiah knew this. He knew the impossible would remain invisible without God in it. That's why he said, "The God of heaven will give us success" (Neh. 2:20). Our plans and goals and dreams are useless without God's direction. "We can make our plans, but the final outcome is in God's hands" (Prov. 16:1 LB).

A leader can delegate many things, but not his faith in God. The faith that produces the plans and dreams for the organization are left to the leader. He or she must lead the way, depending on God for great success.

In reality there are certain factors in our lives that we cannot change. We can't change our parents, our IQs, our personalities. Sometimes we may not be able to change our situations or the people with whom we work. But we can choose the degree of our belief in God. This is the faith factor. And this is the one ingredient that makes or breaks an organization that seeks to make an impact for God and his kingdom. Without it one will never minister on the cutting edge.

William Carey, as mentioned in an earlier chapter, was such a person of faith. Carey left his cobbler's bench in Britain almost two centuries ago to serve as a pioneer missionary in India. He knew no one there; he had no idea what he would face; he had no knowledge of the languages. When he died after more than forty years of ministry in India, he had translated the Bible into three major Indian languages, had founded what has become the largest newspaper in India, had established the strong and effective Baptist Church Union in India, had begun what has become the largest seminary in India, and had done more than any individual to bring the message of the gospel of Christ to that subcontinent. He was one simple cobbler who took God at his word, and his obedience immeasurably affected an entire nation.

May our challenge be: Lead in such a way that we are bound to fail unless God is in it.

ENDNOTES
1. Theodore Roosevelt, quoted in Geoffrey C. Ward, *How Teddy Roosevelt Took Charge!*
2. Winston Churchill, quoted in *The Oxford Dictionary of*

Quotations, 3d ed. (Oxford: Oxford University Press, 1979), 149–150.

3. Stuart Briscoe, quoted in Marshall Shelly, *Well-Intentioned Dragons* (Waco: Word Books, 1985), 35.

4. Roosevelt, address at the Sorbonne, Paris: April 23, 1910, "Citizenship in a Republic," quoted in *The Strenuous Life,* vol. 13 of *The Works of Theodore Roosevelt,* (national ed.: 1926), 510.

5. Roosevelt, quoted in John Bartlett, *Familiar Quotations,* 16th ed., Justin Kaplan, gen. ed. (Boston: Little, Brown and Co., 1992), 575.

9

Integrity—The Light in the Darkness

Steve, a department store executive, felt it was unfair for his merchandise buyers to keep all the clothing samples commonly given away by manufacturers. He directed that the free items be shared with other employees.

One morning Steve arrived at his office and found a sweater on his desk. An attached note from one of the buyers read, "Thought your wife would like this." For an instant, Steve considered keeping the sweater; but he knew he too had to abide by the new policy. He promptly returned the sweater to the buyer, instructing her to give it to a clerk who could not afford such an item.

In the operating room of a large, well-known hospital, a young nurse was completing her first day of full responsibility. "You've only removed eleven sponges, doctor," she said to the surgeon. "We used twelve."

"I removed them all," the doctor declared. "We'll close the incision now."

"No," the nurse objected. "We used twelve sponges."

"I'll take the responsibility," the surgeon said grimly. "Suture!"

"You can't do that!" blazed the nurse. "Think of the patient."

The surgeon smiled, lifted his foot, and showed the nurse the twelfth sponge. "You'll do," he said.[1]

Two friends owned an extremely profitable business. They put it up for sale, and gave their word that, pending a few details, they would sell to a particular buyer. They made this commitment on a Friday. However, over the weekend they received another offer that would have netted them an enormously higher profit.

Unsure of what they should do, they spent the rest of the weekend praying with their wives. By Sunday night they all agreed that their word must be their bond. On Monday morning, they called the second buyer and turned down his better offer.

What do these real life incidents have in common? They speak of the most pressing need in our world today—integrity.

THE MEANING OF INTEGRITY

Integrity is a high standard of living based on a personal code of morality that doesn't succumb to the whim of the moment or the dictates of the majority. Integrity is to personal character what health is to the body. A person of character is whole; his life is put together. People with integrity have nothing to hide and nothing to fear. Their lives are open books.

Integrity is not reputation—what others think of us, nor is it success—what we have accomplished. Integrity embodies the sum total of our being and our actions. It originates with who we are, but it expresses itself in the way we live and behave.

Unfortunately, this trait is in short supply and seems to be diminishing every day. All too frequently integrity is discarded upon the altar of ambition and worldly success. What we want to achieve is more important than what we are to be. The compromise of the personal integrity of governmental leaders, professional entertainers, and religious leaders makes headline news. Others in our midst have lost the handshake of their personal character by succumbing to the whim of the moment for personal gain and private advancement. Integrity is lost when we focus on doing more than on becoming, on expediency more than excellence, on progress rather than purity.

You and I will not stay on the cutting edge without integrity. It is not an option for the believer seeking to make a difference in this world for Christ's sake. Integrity is the absolute standard for a follower of Jesus Christ.

THE MODELS OF INTEGRITY

Without a doubt, Jesus is the supreme model of integrity. His life so evidenced his purity and excellent character that his enemies could only declare, "Teacher, we know you are a man of integrity. You aren't swayed by men, because you pay no attention to who they are; but you teach the way of God in accordance with the truth" (Mark 12:14). At the conclusion of his life here on earth as he stood before Pilate in a mockery of a trial, Pilate said, "I find no basis for a charge against this man" (Luke 23:4). There was no basis for guilt, no evidence of fault, found in Jesus.

The psalmist and king of Israel, David, is often cited as a man of integrity. Of the many references that pay attribute to his blameless and faithful life, one stands out. God spoke to David's son Solomon, "If you walk before me in integrity of heart and uprightness, as David your father did, . . . I will establish your royal throne over Israel forever" (1 Kings 9:4–5). David was not sinless. He was devout and faithful to God. He pursued a life of integrity as the psalms point out (Ps. 7:8, 25:21, 26:1, 41:12). The badge of integrity distinguished his life and leadership.

Centuries later came the destruction of Jerusalem and the exile of her people. When the exiles returned to the beloved city of Jerusalem lead by Nehemiah, the walls of the city were constructed. When the work was completed, a man of integrity named Hanani was given charge over the city. Nehemiah wrote, "I put in charge of Jerusalem my brother Hanani . . . because he was a man of integrity and feared God more than most men do" (Neh. 7:2). This man was placed in a leadership role in part because of his life of integrity.

Another person often associated with patience and persistence was also a man of integrity. We know him by the name of Job. In the midst of Job's suffering, God was the first to speak of his integrity. After Satan had taken everything from Job, God said, "Have you considered my servant Job? There is no one on earth like him; he is blameless and upright, a man who fears God and shuns evil. And he still maintains his integrity, though you incited me against him to ruin him without any reason" (Job 2:3). Later, after Satan had afflicted his body with painful sores from his head to his feet, his wife taunted, "Are you still holding on to your integrity? Curse God and die!" (Job 2:9). Throughout his ordeal Job remained faithful and true to the Lord. In spite of taunts and rebuffs from his friends, he never compromised his integrity: "I will never admit you are in the right; till I die, I will not deny my integrity" (Job 27:5). Job embodied the life of integrity.

Integrity has been modeled for us by these men of faith. Yet for us as contemporary people of faith we need to understand how integrity is manifested in daily living.

THE MANIFESTATION OF INTEGRITY

What are the needed elements for a person to live a life of integrity? What will it take for one's life to be identified with a mark of distinctiveness? While the following ingredients are not all-inclusive, they do provide the foundational framework for a life of integrity.

1. *Conduct yourself in an authentic manner.* The apostle Paul defended his credentials and his apostleship in communicating the message of Christ by stating, "Our conscience testifies that we have conducted ourselves in the world, and especially in our relations with you, in the holiness and *sincerity* that are from God. We have done so not according to worldly wisdom but according to God's grace" (2 Cor. 1:12). In his letter to the Philippians, Paul instructed, "Be *sincere* and blameless until the day of Christ" (Phil. 1:10 NASB). The key word in both of these verses is the word *sincere*.

We use this word all the time. For example, we use it as a complimentary close in our letters, "Sincerely yours." Or when someone tells us they will perform some benefit for us we ask, "Are you sincere?" What is meant by this word?

Sincere is from a Latin word meaning "without wax." The Greek term means "sun-tested."

For a true understanding of this word we must travel back to ancient Italy. In those days, being a sculptor was a popular profession. As in every industry, there was good and bad quality in the statue business. When a sculptor would make a mistake in carving a statue, dishonest merchants would smear pearly-white wax over the cracks, which would pass for the real thing. Sculptors became so good at "remolding" with wax, that most people could not tell the difference in quality with the naked eye. The only way of detecting the flaw and its coverup was by holding the object up to the light of the sun.

If anyone wanted an authentic statue of fine quality, carved by someone who took pride in his work, he would go to the artisan marketplace in the Quad in Rome and look for the signs at the booth mark *sine cera*—"without wax." In the *sine cera* booths one could find the real thing.[2]

Men and women of integrity are those rare and lasting individuals who are the real thing. They have no hidden flaws and cover up no hidden agenda. They are authentic and genuine.

We like working and doing business with people like that. The real question is: Am I that kind of person?

I once read of a real estate salesman who professed to be a Christian. He admitted, "I don't always tell potential buyers facts that might influence their decision negatively. If I were totally true, I'd never make a sale!"

A business manager for a group of newspapers told that he now refuses to grant credit to advertisers whose business cards or stationery bear Christian symbols or Bible verses. His reasoning: Most of his overdue accounts were those of people who boldly proclaimed they were running Christian businesses, yet had not found it necessary to pay for ads they had purchased.

For the Christian leader sincerity is not optional. Jesus' harshest words were directed to the Pharisees—those people he called hypocrites. They were two-faced fakes and counterfeits. We would do well to examine our conduct to make sure we measure up to the exacting standards set by Jesus himself.

2. *Speak the truth always*. Take note of a couple of proverbs. "The LORD detests lying lips, but he delights in men

who are truthful" (Prov. 12:22). "The integrity of the upright guides them, but the unfaithful are destroyed by their duplicity" (Prov. 11:3).

Honesty is a rarity in our day. Perhaps it has always been hard to find. Diogenes, the Greek philosopher, lighted a candle in the daytime and went around looking for an honest man. Blaise Pascal said he didn't expect to meet three honest men in a century. The Institute of Behavior Motivation has found that ninety-seven out of one hundred people tell lies—and they do it about one thousand times a year.

It is sad commentary that in our society retail businesses must resort to lie-detector tests to help select honest clerks and employees. With enough money and the right sources students can buy term papers on any high school or university subject. One can hire a surrogate to take a final exam, one can buy a bachelor's, master's, or doctor's degree. The philosophy of our age seems to be, "Why fail when you can cheat."

But remember that honesty is like a boomerang. Your words, along with who you are, always goes full circle. Every time individuals engage in dishonest activities of any kind the results come back to haunt them. Just ask any politician about skeletons in the closest. Talk to certain tele-evangelists about the boomerang effect.

The person of integrity is different. He or she is of that rare breed of people that fulfill their words. They follow through on commitments. They tell the truth even when it costs.

A salesman was on the brink of retirement and was involved in a potential sale that could net him a hundred thousand dollar commission. Not a bad way to go out. The only problem was, in order to make the deal work he would have to be deceptive when he presented the product to the customer. Would you tell some white lies to earn six figures? But when he considered his integrity he decided to tell the truth. He was honest with the customer, and it cost him the sale.

Was it worth it? You bet it was worth it. Retiring with a clean conscience was a greater reward than a hundred thousand dollar commission.

In the end, speaking the truth always wins out. The

writer of Proverbs says, "The man of integrity walks securely, but he who takes crooked paths will be found out" (Prov. 10:9). When we tell the truth we will not have anything come back and haunt us.

A man became very successful in the real estate brokerage business. A hopeful protegé asked him what had enabled him to excel to such heights.

"I'm just an average, hard-working, honest broker. I'm nothing special," he said. "You see, it's just that the rest of the men in this business cut so many corners that honest and average men like me all of a sudden look great!"

God is looking for men and women of integrity who will be just that—honest.

3. *Stand for what is right.* This is the badge of convictions in the life of a believer. One cannot be a person of integrity without deep convictions. A person with convictions knows what he or she believes and why. Convictions are not forced on an individual; they are beliefs and actions of choice.

Francis Kelley wrote, "Convictions are the mainsprings of action, the driving powers of life. What a man lives are his convictions." Martin Luther King, Jr., often told his children, "If a man has nothing that is worth dying for, then he is not fit to live."

What are you willing to die for? What are you willing to live for?

Conviction must rest on the knowledge of the truth as spelled out in Scripture. Ignorance of God's Word, whatever its cause, is the reason many people have no convictions. The righteous knowledge needed to mold our convictions comes from being intimately acquainted with God's Word. Without the Scripture in our lives we wither like grass in the fires of temptation. Convictionless people do whatever they feel.

Daniel and his three friends were different. They knew exactly what God wanted them to do, or not to do. They had carefully studied the Law of Moses and had gained, by faith, deep convictions on how they should live in the midst of a heathen people. They could stand strong, even when they found themselves completely alone, because of their deep-rooted convictions.

The three friends stood before the fiery furnace. They had

refused to fall down and worship the golden image erected by Nebuchadnezzar. They didn't know what would happen to them. Yet they were deeply convinced that they must, in complete obedience, do what God's Law said, whatever the consequences. In response to the King's demand to worship the golden image, the three men answered:

"If it be so, our God whom we serve is able to deliver us from the furnace of blazing fire; and he will deliver us out of your hand, O king. But even if he does not, let it be known to you, O king, that we are not going to serve your gods or worship the golden image that you have set up" (Dan. 3:17–18 NASB).

These words were spoken by men with deep spiritual convictions. How would you have responded? Would you have rationalized or justified falling down to this heathen image? Would you have compromised your beliefs, your convictions? Or would you have stood tall and pronounced boldly as the three Jews, "No way, King Nebuchadnezzar, we will serve only the Lord God. He will protect us. Even if he doesn't we will gladly die for his sake."

In the movie *Chariots of Fire* I was inspired by Eric Liddell's conviction not to run on Sunday. His was a conviction forged out of a strong belief in the biblical law of remembering "the sabbath day to keep it holy" (Ex. 20:8 NASB). He had trained diligently for this track event but now his Olympic hopes were crumbling. Was his desire and hope to end in ashes? No. He entered another event. He had not prepared for it, but was allowed to compete. Victory looked impossible. Then, just before the race, one of the contestants put a note in Eric's hand: "He who honors me, I will honor." Eric ran in faith. His convictions were intact. He honored God. And God honored him. Eric Liddell won the gold medal.

People of integrity sometimes have no choice but to cling to their convictions, look to the Lord, and refuse to compromise their faith. Fred, a high school teacher, felt it was his duty before God to teach the biblical view of Creation as well as the theory of evolution. This often gave him an opportunity to present the gospel to individuals in his class. Eventually one parent, incensed to learn her son had prayed to accept Jesus Christ, demanded that the principal prohibit the teacher from "imposing his faith on young, impressionable people."

The principal ordered Fred not to teach about Creation or to talk about his Christian faith in the classroom. Fred did not argue, but the next time he taught the theory of evolution he again presented the scriptural account of Creation. Fred was soon confronted by the principal and fired.

In the quest for integrity, convictions are prerequisite. We must know what we believe. We must determine what we will stand for, and if called upon, what we will die for.

As one can see, there is more to integrity than we might have thought at first. Integrity goes much deeper than just what we do or think. It is that intangible quality that will some day summarize our lives.

Billy Graham, speaking to a world conference of national evangelists, declared that our world today is looking for men and women of integrity. Several months later in an interview, the word popped up again; "Graham says he will be content with a simple epitaph for his life and ministry: 'A sinner saved by grace; a man who, like the psalmist, walked in his integrity. I'd like people to remember that I had integrity.'"[3]

When you die, what will the people standing around your grave say about you? Will they comment, "He was authentic, genuine, real"? Will they say, "She told the truth and fulfilled her word"? Will they say, "He stood for what is right"? Will they add, "She could be trusted"? Will they say, "He was honest"? In other words, could they write on your gravestone, Here lies a person of integrity?

ENDNOTES

1. Denis Waitley, *Being the Best* (Nashville: Oliver Nelson, 1987), 51.

2. Winston Churchill, quoted in Waitley, *Seeds of Greatness* (Old Tappan, N.J.: Revell, 1983), 84.

3. Billy Graham, interview by Bruce Buursma, "Concerns of the Evangelist," *Christianity Today*, 29, no. 6 (5 April 1985): 22.

10

Passion—*Giving One's Life for Eternity*

For twelve years the Green Bay Packers had won only thirty percent of their games, and in 1958 their record dropped to a dismal one and ten. Then in 1959 came a new coach—Vince Lombardi. During Lombardi's nine-year reign the Packers had nine winning seasons, beat their opponents seventy-five percent of the time, and walked away with five NFL championships, including the first two Super Bowls. What caused the turnaround? Perhaps Bart Starr, the former quarterback who was there when Lombardi came, will give us insight into what made the coach tick. Starr said:

"I wasn't mentally tough before I met Coach Lombardi. I hadn't reached the point where I refused to accept second best. I was too nice at times. I don't believe that nice guys necessarily finish last. I think what Leo Durocher really meant is that nice guys don't finish first. To win, you have to have a certain amount of mental toughness. Coach Lombardi gave me that. He taught me that you must have a flaming desire to win. It's got to dominate all your waking hours. It can't ever wane. It's got to glow in you all the time."[1]

"It's got to glow in you," Starr says. What glows? Passion,

the flaming desire to win. And it glows "all the time." That's probably an impossibility. But even in his exaggeration, Bart Starr is telling us something of the curious stuff within people who want to be a part of the extraordinary in the world, the folk who change things, the leaders who move people and do great things for God.

And so we should. Christian leaders have good reason to be the most passionate people on earth. We are, after all, loved and accepted by God. We are forgiven by Christ's atoning work on the cross. We are empowered and unleashed in ministry by the Holy Spirit.

IGNITED BY A FIRE

Passion, like the wind, is sometimes difficult to define. Duke Ellington, the late jazz musician, composer, and renowned band leader, provided a definition of rhythm that also applies to passion. "If you got it," he said, "you don't need no definition. And if you don't have it, ain't no definition gonna help."[2] In its essence, passion is the fuel that fires our meaningfulness, the force that drives the soul, the burden that compels the individual. People move beyond ordinary human activities because of it. People rise to the top of business, sports, academia, science, politics, and ministry because they are ignited by it. Some of those people explode like a Molotov cocktail to inflame a whole generation. Others burn quietly in the furnaces of everyday life, unknown to all but their immediate acquaintances—yet making a difference in their world. Ferdinand Foch was right when he stated, "The most powerful weapon on earth is the human soul on fire."

People with passion rise above mediocrity and the mundane. They tackle seemingly overwhelming obstacles and are tireless in their pursuits. They often pay incredible prices to reach a certain goal as if an undying flame keeps them burning. They endure suffering and hardship to excel. Michael Meyer, writing in *The Alexander Complex*, says, "What distinguishes the empire builders in the end is their passion. They devote their lives to an idea that in time becomes an ideal. More important, they inspire others to buy into their dream. All are out, in one way or another, to change the world."[3] The French author Diderot adds, "Only passions, great passions, can elevate the soul to great things."[4] And as it relates to ministry, Charles Spurgeon, in *Lectures to My Students*, observed that, "In many instances, ministerial success is traceable almost entirely to an intense zeal, a consuming passion for souls, and an eager enthusiasm in the cause of God, and we believe that in every case, other things being equal, men prosper in the divine service in proportion as their hearts are blazing with holy love."[5]

While putting a finger on the definition may prove elusive, certain characteristics are evident in the lives of people fueled by the fires of passion.

COMMITTED TO CHANGING THEIR WORLD

Passionate people are focused on making a difference where they are. Their immediate attention is closely confined, but often it bleeds into the fabric of society at large. Their attitude most often is: While I can't change the whole world I can make a difference in my town, or my business, or my church.

I think the mother was operating from passion when she said that her mission in life was to raise children who would love Christ. With tear-filled eyes, this mother, now in her nineties, talked about her godly daughter, who married a pastor and helped him start a powerful suburban church. And she spoke of her son, a businessman who had witnessed dozens of other professional people come to Christ. She changed her world.

I think of a Sunday school teacher who lacked a great deal of formal education and biblical knowledge, but he loved his class. Each Sunday he made us feel special as his eyes twinkled when he told the story of Jesus. He reminded us each week that he was praying for us. He had a great hope in us. While all the boys in that class did not become missionaries or evangelists or preachers one of us did. Passionately, in his own way, this teacher changed the world.

Nehemiah, the right-hand man for King Artaxerxes of Persia, requested permission to return to his homeland to help rebuild the wall around Jerusalem. He wrote, "I went to Jerusalem, and after staying there three days I set out during the night with a few men. I had not told anyone *what my God had put in my heart* to do for Jerusalem" (Neh. 2:11–

12). What was God putting in his heart? God was stoking the fires of passion that would enable Nehemiah to lead a ragtag bunch of people to rebuild a massive wall that encircled an entire city, while encountering verbal attacks of criticism and much opposition. Yet with overwhelming odds stacked against them, they accomplished the feat. "So the wall was completed . . . in fifty-two days. When all our enemies heard about this, all the surrounding nations were afraid and lost their self-confidence, because they realized that this work had been done with the help of our God" (Neh. 6:15–16). Nehemiah, fueled with passion, changed his world.

The apostle Paul stated his world-changing passion when he wrote, "It has always been my ambition to preach the gospel where Christ was not known, so that I would not be building on someone else's foundation" (Rom. 15:20). Paul's all-consuming passion was to reach spiritually dead people with the life-giving power of the good news of Christ. It consumed and motivated his entire life, giving him the burning embers to endure all sorts of pain and injustice. He crisscrossed the known world of that time planting churches, winning people to Christ, and edifying the saints, to see his mission accomplished. And in the end, while not every person had been reached and not every city boasted a Christian church, Paul could truthfully proclaim, "I was not disobedient to the vision from heaven" (Acts 26:19). Paul, fueled with the fires of passion, changed his world.

Suffice it to say that passion entails change. Passion is never about maintaining the status quo. It is about stretching reality to extend beyond the existing state, rising to a new level.

SINGULARLY FOCUSED

J. C. Ryle wrote about people fueled with the fire of passion in his spiritual classic, *Holiness*. For passion, he used its synonym, zeal. And in his words we find another characteristic of a passionate person. "Zeal in religion is a burning desire to please God, to do his will, and to advance his glory in the world in every possible way. . . . A zealous man in religion is preeminently a man of one thing."[6]

Men and women of passion are able to boil their purpose down to a single desire and focus their lives entirely to that end. That action embodies the secret of much of their drive, if not their success. In a world of compromise and vacillation, of distractions and multiple options, passion-filled people recognize that single-mindedness is a precious, needed quality for ministering on the cutting edge.

Take Jesus for example. His life was full of difficult choices that called for sacrificing good things for the better. At the height of his popularity with the multitudes, he forsook favor with the people in order to ordain twelve ordinary men to the ministry. He was opposed at various times by every segment of society, including his own friends, relatives, and personally-ordained disciples. But he stood steadfast in his God-given objectives. He was never sidetracked.

With a singularly focused passion rooted in the principles of God's Word, we can be fashioned into useful tools that can move people to influence the world for Christ. There comes a time when we must tenaciously choose the course we will go, or the relentless drift of events, meetings, and other people will make the decision for us. Perhaps the time for us is now. The psalmist wrote, "Teach me your way, O LORD, and I will walk in your truth; give me an undivided heart, that I may fear your name" (Ps. 86:11).

NOT AFRAID TO FAIL

Passionate people fail and fail often. They are not born winners nor does everything they touch turn to gold. They have tasted the dirt of defeat. They have been embraced in the arms of failure. But they always get up and keep trying. They may be knocked down but they are never knocked out. They may fall down but they don't stay down.

Seneca said, "If thou art a man, admire those who attempt great things, even though they fail." Theodore Roosevelt remarked, "The only man who never makes a mistake is the man who never does anything." We should probably examine our lives if we have not experienced a few flops recently. If we are not failing now and again, it is a sure sign we are playing it safe, not playing on the cutting edge. "Failure never hurt anybody," Jack Lemmon once said. "It's the fear of failure that kills you, that kills artists [and leaders]. You've got to go down that alley and take those chances."[7]

People fueled with the fire of passion have come to expect failure, experience failure, and use failure as a springboard to fulfill their cause. Imagine, for instance, how easy it would have been for this young man to have bowed his head and given up. He failed in business in '31, he was defeated for the legislature in '32, he was elected to the legislature in '34. His sweetheart died in '35, he had a nervous breakdown in '36, he was defeated for speaker in '38, he was defeated for elector in '40, he was defeated for Congress in '43, he was elected to Congress in '46, defeated for Congress in '48, defeated for the Senate in '50, defeated for vice president in '56, and for the Senate in '58. That would be enough to make most people give up. But a passionate flame to make a difference in the world glowed like campfire embers within his soul. At times it seemed that the fire was doused. But the determination to go on was ever-present. Even when the night looked the darkest, a glimmer of light peeked through the recesses of discouragement and despair to keep the passion aglow. And I, for one, am thankful it did. Because, fortunately enough, that man was elected president of the United States in 1860. His name was Abraham Lincoln.

John Westfall, in his wonderful book *Coloring Outside The Lines*, writes, "Passion grows best in an atmosphere where we are granted the freedom to fail as well as to succeed."[8] Passionate people know that success may be around the next bend in the road. They know that it is always too soon to quit. The attainment of dreams and long-awaited goals often comes on the heels of multiple and repeated failures.

GIVE THEMSELVES TO A GREATER CAUSE

William James, the author of *The Varieties of Religious Experience*, wrote, "The best use of your life is to invest it in something that will out last it." All too often we give ourselves to causes and ventures that will wither and die when we die. Passionate people have learned a secret—that their lives are best used when they are devoted to a cause, a project, a dream that is bigger than themselves and will live on after they are dead and gone.

Martin Luther, a Catholic priest disturbed by what he witnessed in the Catholic church and enlightened by what he was reading in Holy Scripture, nailed his ninety-five theses on the Wittenburg chapel door. He stood before the intimidating power of the papal legates from Rome and proclaimed, "Here I stand; I can do nothing else." The Christian church is where it is today because this one man was willing to give himself to something bigger than himself.

Martin Luther King, Jr., was a Baptist preacher in the south. While he was regarded as a powerful orator, nothing in his background—academic prowess, family connections, political skills, or church growth statistics—indicated that he was an emerging leader, a crusader to be reckoned with. However, King had a dream—a dream of racial equality and justice. God began to work through King to mold and make him into a servant with a larger calling. Because one man was willing to give himself to something bigger than himself we live in a much different world today.

Yet people with passion don't always have to make headlines or be burned at the stake for their causes. Many passionate people grind out their dreams in the mills of everyday life. They are teachers and parents, coaches and preachers. They are men and women committed to a family, or to a class, or to a congregation. Their struggle may not make it to the nightly news, but their sweat and toil will one day come to fruition in the lives of a son or a daughter or a student or a church member. And when all is said and done, their passionate commitment may be the most highly recognized in the annals of eternity.

WHAT'S YOUR PASSION?

At one time or another, if we want to make a difference in our world we must wrestle with some scrappy questions: What are we committed to for life? What is the singular purpose of our lives and ministries? What would we do if we knew we couldn't fail? What are we giving ourselves to that will live longer than we will? What fuels the fire of our lives?

If you are unsure, and would like to strike the flint that

will ignite the spark of passion, let me suggest that you ask yourself the following questions:

What would God have me to do? First and foremost, we need to get direction and guidance from God. Without his input we will become like a wildfire, potentially powerful, but completely out of control. And the only way to hear from God is to spend time alone with God. The psalmist wrote, "Be still, and know that I am God" (Ps. 46:10). This first question is too big and too important to address to God at those times spent alone in the car barreling down the freeway. The question necessitates that we spend quality time alone with the Father. Paul spent three years alone with God in the desert of Arabia before he began the thrust of his ministry activity. For me, at least, I don't need to spend three years alone with God, I need to spend a lifetime alone with God, requesting his direction. Passion most often is not static, but a fluid drive that flows like a river downstream. Time spent with God keeps the stream flowing within the proper channels.

What am I good at? When we identify our gifts and talents we get a clue as to what objective our passion should take. God uses our gifts to indicate what we are to do. How silly it would be for God to grant us certain gifts only to ask us to perform a task or accomplish a mission that we lack the necessary skills and equipment to complete. When I stand before God, he is not going to ask me why wasn't I Bill Hybels or Rick Warren or Billy Graham. All he wants from me is that I be me, that I use the gifts and talents he has entrusted to me in order to accomplish the purpose he has given me to do.

What have I learned? Next, we must review our experiences. In each life difficulties arise. In each life there are hurts and pains that can be learning experiences for us and guiding experiences for others when we share what we have learned. God never promised that we would be trouble free. Hardships are a part of life. But from those troubles and hurts and the principles we learn from them, we can be in a better position to help others.

For example, I was visiting a prospective church member recently with a man in our congregation that had liver cancer. As we drove to our appointment he told me how people don't talk to him about his cancer. "It's almost as if people are afraid of saying the wrong words," he said. Then my friend leaned over and said to me, "If you ever need someone to go with you to talk with someone that has cancer, I'll be glad to go with you. I know their language. I can talk to them. I've been there before." This man had taken his experience, learned from it, and now was willing to be used by God to help those who are struggling through a similar pain. This man had learned what passionate people learn: God never wastes a hurt or a circumstance. He can take the pain of our lives and use it to accomplish something good.

What's going to last the longest? We need to decide what is truly important. The Bible tells us that only two things will last forever: God's word and God's people. Whatever our passion, if it does not include God's word and people, then it is futile. Our passion, for it to be a God-honoring passion, must deal with these two eternal objects.

When am I going to start? Passionate people translate their devotion into action. They discover, as we must, that a passion unchanneled soon dissipates.

At great expense and effort, the famed British preacher Leslie Weatherhead came to speak at an evangelistic rally in the United States. The crowd was large. They were expecting a long and marvelous message from this great man of God. After the preliminaries, he slowly walked to the podium. He surveyed the congregation with his eyes of steel. He thundered in his rich baritone voice, "Do you have it? (Pause.) Will you share it? (Pause.) When in God's name are you going to start?" Then quietly, as the audience felt the sting of his words, he returned to his seat. His message was finished.

The spark that ignites the fuel of our lives was meant to thrust us into action. If we have it, then, in the words of Leslie Weatherhead, "When in God's name are we going to start?"

ENDNOTES

1. Bart Starr, quoted in Jerry Kramer, ed., *Lombardi: Winning Is The Only Thing* (New York: Pocket Books, 1970), 86.

2. Edward "Duke" Ellington, quoted in Barna, *The Power of Vision* (Ventura: Regal Books, 1992), 28.

3. Michael Meyer, *The Alexander Complex* (New York: Times Books, 1989), xiii.

4. Denis Diderot, quoted in John F. Westfall, *Coloring Outside the Lines* (New York: HarperCollins, 1991), 123.

5. Charles H. Spurgeon, *Lectures to My Students* (Grand Rapids: Zondervan, 1972), 305.

6. J. C. Ryle, *Holiness* (Grand Rapids: Evangelical Press, 1956), 35.

7. Jack Lemmon, quoted in Alan Loy McGinnis, *Bringing Out the Best in People* (Minneapolis: Augsburg Publishing House, 1985), 75.

8. Westfall, *Coloring Outside the Lines*, 130.

11

Remaining on the Cutting Edge

Apple Computer was struggling and Steve Jobs, its founder, had decided John Sculley was the man needed to pump new life into the company. Jobs made numerous trips to New York to persuade Sculley to leave Pepsi Cola, where he was the head of one of the divisions of the company.

The crucial conversation occurred high over the city as the two men took in the view of the New York skyline from a picture window in a skyscraper. Steve Jobs put the question to Sculley, "Will you come?" Sculley responded, "I thought it all through, and I just can't. Financially, you'd have to give me a million dollar salary, a million dollar sign-up bonus, and a million dollars severance if it doesn't work out."

Jobs asked him, "How did you come up with those numbers?" And Sculley responded, "They are just big round numbers!"

Jobs persisted, and Sculley resisted and made a counter offer to be a consultant. Jobs then confronted him with this: "Do you want to spend the rest of your life selling sugared water, or do you want a chance to change the world?"

It was a pivotal point for Sculley. It knocked the wind out of him. He went to Apple Computer.[1]

Have you ever wanted to change the world? To make a difference? To leave this world better than you found it?

Very few people begin life saying, "I want to change the world." Even people who have left an undeniable mark on this world rarely set out to make that difference. Yet there are windows of time in one's life when one has the power to change things. These times are pivotal points. At our moment of decision we can drift back into the doldrums or march boldly into the future.

Perhaps you are at one of those moments, a pivotal point. Perhaps this book has awakened in you a sleeping giant of a dream or a desire of something you have wanted to accomplish in your ministry. What will it take for you and me to change the world? To make that difference? What must we do at our pivotal points?

DARE TO BE DIFFERENT

Only in daring to be different can a difference be made. Only when individuals change can the world be changed. When we have mustered the courage, then we must get out of our ruts and try something new.

Jean-Claude Killy captured virtually every major skiing trophy in 1966 and 1967. The next year he won three gold medals in the Winter Olympics, a record in ski racing that has never been topped. How did he do that? It was not that he worked harder than anyone else. Each person on the French National Ski Team was prepared to work harder to be the best. Killy realized instinctively that simply training harder would never be enough. Killy then began challenging the basic theories of racing technique. Each week he would try something different to see if he could find a better, faster way down the mountain.

His experiments resulted in a new style that was almost exactly the opposite of the accepted technique of the time. It involved skiing with his legs apart for better balance and sitting back on the skis when he came to a turn. He also used ski poles in an unorthodox way to propel himself as he skied. The explosive new style helped cut Killy's racing times dramatically.[2]

Perhaps you have looked at a new way of doing a certain task. Perhaps you have thought of a new approach to an old problem. Perhaps you have discovered a new slant to accomplishing a certain project. Why not give it a try? Dare to put your different approach to the test.

Now remember, not everyone wants you and me to be different. They like things the way they have always been. They are content with the status quo—the dull edge of life and ministry. They are change-killers. They are present each time you and I want to make a difference. They speak their subtle words. When faced with a pivotal point, a moment of decision, they want us to take the path of least resistance. Their statements usually begin with one of the four following remarks:

Tradition. "We've never done it that way before." We should not deny our heritage, but let's not bury ourselves in the past either. Tradition is a reflection of the past; changing the world is a reflection of the future. The two should be married. We must honor our past by incorporating past strengths into our future.

Fear. "I'm afraid of anything new." Remaining on the cutting edge means breaking out of comfort zones, doing new things, or operating in areas where we lack a proven track record. Change can be scary. But this is where faith comes in.

Complacency. "It doesn't matter what we do." Remaining on the cutting edge requires the giving of all you've got, laying everything on the line. No successful business grew by waiting for business to come to them. No best-selling author waited for publishers to approach him. No great salesperson sat idly by waiting for people to show up at the door so he or she could sell the product.

Fatigue. "I'm tired. I've done my part. Let someone else do the work now." Staying on the edge is not easy. It requires a great deal of energy. And if possible we should be well rested before we take on a significant task. But usually the people who make a difference are tired. The world changer Jesus was able to sleep on a boat while going through a storm. The world has always been changed by tired people.

A world changer must possess more than an innate desire to be different. He or she must also have a desire to make things happen.

WILLING TO ACT

History is replete with men and women who changed the world because they dared to get involved and do something. World changers are people of action, they make things happen.

The naturalist Loren Eisley, visiting a seaside town, spent his early morning hours walking along a beach. Each day at sunrise he found townspeople combing the sand for starfish to kill and sell for commercial purposes. It was for Eisley a sign of all the ways the world says no to life.

But one morning, he got up unusually early and discovered a solitary figure on the beach. This man, too, was gathering starfish, but each time he found one alive, he would pick it up and throw it as far as he could, back into the ocean from which it came. As days went by Eisley found this man embarked on his mission each morning, seven days a week, regardless of weather.

One day Eisley approached the "star thrower" and asked, "Why are you throwing starfish back into the water?"

"Isn't it obvious?" the star thrower replied.

"Yes," said Eisley, "but the ocean is so big and the beach is so long and there are so many starfish. What difference can you possibly make?"

As the star thrower picked up another starfish to hurl it back into the ocean, he replied, "It will make a difference for this one."

To change the world one must choose not to be an observer but an actor, not a watcher but a doer, not a spectator but a player.

Are you at a pivotal point? Are you reaching down to pick up a starfish? Will you hurl it in the right direction? In the whole scheme of things our efforts may not seem that significant, but they will make a difference for our world.

The popular business seminar leader Joel Barker says, "Vision without action is a dream. Action without vision is a waste of time. Vision with action can change the world." You and I can change the world. We can dare to be different, and reach down and rescue our starfish.

Prior to 1967, the Swiss controlled more than eighty percent of the wristwatch market. But that year a new watch, powered by a quartz crystal, was introduced. This marvelous watch was invented by a Swiss watchmaker. He took the idea to his supervisors who told him to forget it. It would never sell. The Swiss rejected it. In fact, the Swiss executives thought the quartz watch was such a ludicrous idea that they didn't even patent it. They were at a pivotal point. They forgot a fundamental principle of their business: their task was not to make watches, but to provide people a way to tell time.

Their failure to act, to seize this window of opportunity, cost them dearly. Texas Instruments of America and Seiko of Japan picked up on the quartz idea, and the rest is history. This new quartz-powered watch swept the market. And today the Swiss produce less than five percent of the world's watches. Prior to 1967 there were more than sixty-five thousand Swiss watchmakers. Today there are fewer than fifteen thousand.

EXPECT THE BLESSINGS OF GOD

Leaders on the cutting edge have a desire to be different, the courage to act, and the hope of God's favor. If I could describe your situation and God's response to it, it might read something like this:

> You are at the right place, at the right moment in history, to accomplish great things for the kingdom of God. This is the pivotal moment, the window of opportunity. Such a time might never come again. You must believe that.
>
> God has placed his hand upon you. He has prepared you for this pivotal moment with the necessary equipment and endowments to do great things. Your unique blend of gifts and talents will assist you to accomplish a world-changing cause. You must believe that.
>
> Don't misunderstand. I'm not saying that your task will be easy. I'm not implying that your venture will be free from pain and adversity. You must be prepared to sacrifice and toil hard whether anyone else does or not. You must believe that.
>
> God in his graciousness and goodness has brought you to this point to make a difference in your world. It would be outside the boundaries of God's character

to give you a burning passion, a great vision, and commitment to making a difference, only to turn his back on you. That is not in God's nature nor is it a part of his plan. To deny the intended blessings of God would be like knocking his hand away and slapping him in the face. God's blessings are ready to be lavished upon you. You must believe that.

Today you are at that juncture—a pivotal point. Please don't miss this opportunity. Will you spend the rest of your life doing business as usual, or will you change the world? Will you be content to live on the dull edge of apathy, or will you invest your life on the cutting edge of ministry? The crucial choice is yours.

ENDNOTES

1. John Sculley, *Odyssey* (New York: Harper and Row, 1987), 90.

2. *The Pastor's Story File*, vol. 8, (Platteville, Colo.: Saratoga Press, 1991), 2.

Bibliography

Barna, George. *The Frog In The Kettle*. Ventura, Calif.: Regal Books, 1990.

Bartlett, John. *Familiar Quotations*. 16th ed. Justin Kaplan, ed. Boston: Little, Brown and Co., 1992.

Briscoe, Stuart. Quoted in Marshall Shelley. *Well-Intentioned Dragons*. Waco: Word Books, 1985.

Churchill, Winston. Quoted in Denis Waitley. *Seeds of Greatness*. Old Tappan, N.J.: Revell, 1983.

Covey, Stephen R. *The Seven Habits of Highly Effective People*. New York: Simon and Schuster, 1989.

Diderot, Denis. Quoted in John F. Westfall. *Coloring Outside the Lines*. New York: HarperCollins, 1991.

Ellington, Edward "Duke." Quoted in Barna. *The Power of Vision*. Ventura, Calif.: Regal Books, 1992.

Engstrom, Ted W. *The Pursuit of Excellence*. Grand Rapids: Zondervan, 1982.

Graham, Billy. Interview by Bruce Buursma. "Concerns of the Evangelist." *Christianity Today* 29, no. 6 (5 april 1985): 22.

Gray, E. M. "The Common Denominator of Success." Quoted in Stephen R. Covey. *The Seven Habits of Highly Effective People* (New York: Simon and Schuster, 1989).

Halverson, Richard C. Quoted in Edward R. Dayton and Ted W. Engstrom. *Strategy for Living.* Ventura, Calif.: Regal Books, 1976.

Hansel, Tim. *When I Relax I Feel Guilty.* Elgin, Ill.: LifeJourney Books, 1979.

Havner, Vance. *The Secret of Christian Joy.* Philadelphia: Pinebrook Book Club, 1938.

Hewett, James S., ed. *Illustrations Unlimited.* Wheaton: Tyndale, 1988.

Hovey, E. Paul. *The Treasury of Inspirational Anecdotes, Quotations, and Illustrations.* Grand Rapids: Revell, 1959.

James, William. *The Varieties of Religious Experience.* New York: The Modern Library, 1902.

Kami, Michael J. *Trigger Points.* New York: MacGraw Hill, 1988.

Kelly, Thomas R. *A Testament of Devotion.* New York: Harper and Brothers Publishers, 1941.

Lemmon, Jack. Quoted in Alan Loy McGinnis. *Bringing Out the Best in People.* Minneapolis: Augsburg Publishing House, 1985.

Littleton, Mark R. *Delighted By Discipline.* Wheaton: Victor Books, 1990.

MacArthur, John. *The Ultimate Priority.* Chicago: Moody Press, 1983.

Marx, Karl. Quoted in Robert Coleman. *The Master Plan of Evangelism.* Old Tappan, N.J.: Spire Books, 1963.

Means, James E. *Effective Pastors for a New Century*. Grand Rapids: Baker Books, 1993.

Meyer, Michael. *The Alexander Complex*. New York: Times Books, 1989.

Palau, Luis. *Dream Great Dreams*. Portland, Oreg.: Multnomah Press, 1984.

Platt, Suzy, ed. *Respectfully Quoted*. Washington, D.C.: Library of Congress, 1989.

Powell, Paul W. *Go-Givers in a Go-Getter World*. Nashville: Broadman Press, 1986.

Ryle, J. C. *Holiness*. Grand Rapids: Evangelical Press, 1956.

Sculley, John. *Odyssey*. New York: Harper and Row, 1987.

Spurgeon, Charles H. *Lectures to My Students*. Grand Rapids: Zondervan, 1972.

Starr, Bart. Quoted in Jerry Kramer, ed. *Lombardi: Winning Is The Only Thing*. New York: Pocket Books, 1970.

Swindoll, Charles R. *Living Above the Level of Mediocrity*. Waco: Word Books, 1987.

Taylor, Jack R. *Much More*. Nashville: Broadman Press, 1972.

The Oxford Dictionary of Quotations. 3d ed. Oxford: Oxford University Press, 1979.

The Pastor's Story File. vol. 8. Platteville, Colo.: Saratoga Press, 1991.

Tozer, A. W. *Worship: The Missing Jewel*. Camp Hill, Pa.: Christian Publications, 1992.

Waitley, Denis. *Being The Best*. Nashville: Oliver Nelson, 1987.

Weber, Robert E. *Worship Is A Verb*. Waco: Word Books, 1985.